CREATING A

Cottage Garden

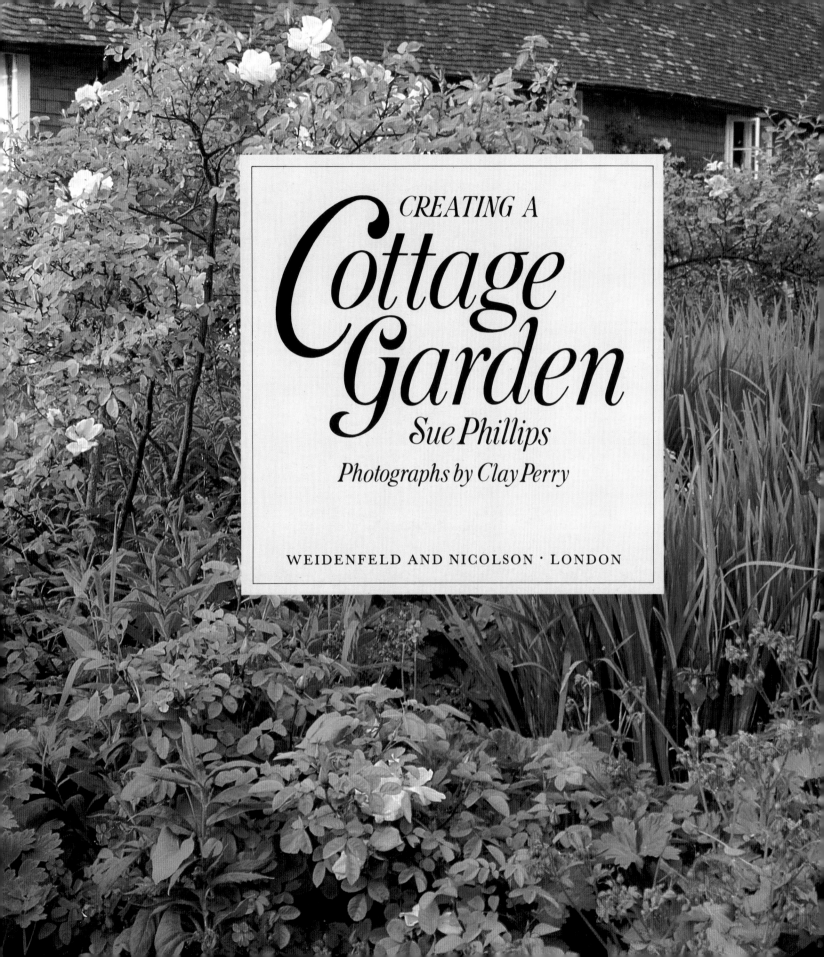

CREATING A

Cottage Garden

Sue Phillips

Photographs by Clay Perry

WEIDENFELD AND NICOLSON · LONDON

First published in Great Britain in 1990 by
George Weidenfeld & Nicolson Limited
91 Clapham High Street, London SW4 7TA

Designed by Harry Green
Artwork by John Wyer

Colour separations by Newsele Litho Ltd
Filmset by Keyspools Ltd, Golborne, Lancs
Printed and bound in Italy by L.E.G.O., Vicenza

Contents

Introduction

~

After many years of low-maintenance gardening – all shrubs and ground-cover plants – fashion has turned full circle and gardeners' gardening has once again come back into favour. Now, people are less concerned about finding ways to cut down the work, and more interested in giving their gardens character and individuality, and in making them suitable homes for all sorts of fascinating and unusual plants.

This change in emphasis has led to a great revival of interest in garden history, and in resurrecting gardening styles of the past. And one of the most pleasing of these to benefit from the nostalgia boom is traditional cottage gardening. Today, thousands of people, inspired by gardens they've seen at big flower shows, on TV programmes, or when garden visiting in pretty rural villages, want to create a country cottage garden for themselves. So where do you start? What goes into a cottage garden? And how do you capture the romance that is such an important part of a real cottage garden?

Although the best cottage gardens look deceptively simple, in practice they are not so easy to create – unless you have a well-versed mentor for guidance. The secrets of creating a cottage garden are best discovered by talking to people who have already done it successfully, and by looking at the results they have achieved. In this way, you discover which plants to grow, what architectural features to use, and how to put them all together to make a garden that looks as if it just 'happened' naturally, without the help of considerable planning or even a planting scheme.

You don't need a quaint old-world cottage in order to practise the art of cottage gardening – it's really much more to do with attitude of mind. Take a blend of useful and ornamental plants, including sweet-scented herbs, old-fashioned flowers, ornamental vegetables, roses, climbers, and an old fruit tree or two, plus evocative extras like arches, arbours, old brick paths, stone sinks, or Victorian terracotta forcing pots, add a little of the old cottagers' magic, and you are well on the way!

In writing this book, I have visited a huge selection of very different cottage gardens and asked their owners to share the expertise they have gained the hard way – by finding out for themselves – to help other people create cottage gardens that 'work'. And whether you are planning to start a cottage garden from scratch, modify an existing garden or just enjoy visiting other peoples' gardens, I hope you will discover through these pages something of the lure of cottage gardening that keeps its devotees constantly fascinated.

What is a real Cottage Garden?

You can still see what a real, old cottage garden looked like in illustrations found in old books on gardening, cottages, or country life, or in Victorian and Edwardian watercolours.

The traditional cottage garden had a straight path leading up to the front door through 'wall-to-wall' borders filled with plants. The path might be edged with scallop shells or large pebbles and beside them a neat row of plants such as double daisies created a formal framework. Beyond this grew a tangled mass of rampant plants like gardener's garters, bluebells, primroses, bachelor's buttons and self-sown annuals, punc-

tuated perhaps by the occasional, oddly formal row of crown imperials. From the front door of the cottage almost hidden by a climber-clad porch, an earth or cinder path led round to the back of the house. The back garden, a century or so ago, would almost certainly have contained a mixture of livestock, poultry, bees, herbs and vegetables, fruit trees and bushes, with perhaps a few flowers.

A straight copy of a real early cottage garden would probably not be very acceptable to the cottage gardener of today. The genuine article was not as pretty as we would want our surroundings to be. Ornamental planting has become more important, as self-sufficiency has been less essential. Fashions in gardening have changed too. Many of the features found in the most attractive cottage gardens now, have in fact been 'borrowed' from the old gardens of the wealthy gentry rather than from those of the cottagers. Nor does a real cottage garden make a good home for the delicate 'treasures' we like to grow nowadays, which need special care and attention, unlike the robust and invasive old cottage favourites that could be left to look after themselves. We also require functional features such as garages and garden sheds, and ornamental ones like container gardens and lawns that would have been impractical for early cottagers to take care of. But there are styles of planting and kinds of features which evoke the old-fashioned cottage garden of the past, while still accommodating our lifestyles today. Now, whether you live in an old-world cottage with a thatched roof, lead-glazed mullioned windows, and a rustic porch over which winter jasmine and roses grow, or in a modern town house, it is possible to have a cottage garden.

The front garden of this 15th-century cottage at Ditchling,
East Sussex, is mainly devoted to old-fashioned roses.
Twenty-five different varieties grow amid a patchwork of
old-fashioned ground-hugging plants, in a space no
bigger than the average front garden.

1

Spring

~

Early Flowers and Young Leaves

Cottage gardens are at their picturesque best in midsummer, when the traditional roses, annuals and herbaceous flowers are in riotous bloom. However, a garden based mainly on summer flowers can look very dull for the rest of the year. It is asking rather a lot of any garden, cottage or otherwise, to look outstandingly good all the year round, but there is a second 'high season' – in spring – when cottage gardens can also put on a spectacular show.

This very simple spring garden of winter jasmine, aubrieta, primroses and polyanthus, narcissi and hellebores at a cottage in Oxfordshire, looks very natural. The predominately yellow colour scheme ensures the flowers stand out well from the background, creating pinpricks of light in a rather shady corner.

In spring, the most frequently seen view of the garden will be from indoors, so it is particularly important to plan spring attraction that forms a picture framed by the living-room windows. In this small Oxfordshire garden, the spring flowers have been concentrated into specific areas – under the flowering cherry, and in the border on the opposite side of the garden. A discreetly placed pot plant indoors provides a natural link to the garden beyond.

Planning a Spring Garden

Given a garden of half an acre (0.2 hectares) or more, it is comparatively easy to find room for enough early-flowering plants to create a complete spring garden. But in a very small plot it is much more difficult to do so without sacrificing space that is needed for summer plants. Under these circumstances it can be tempting to dot spring-flowering plants around wherever there is room. However, you achieve a much better effect if you concentrate your resources in a few strategically placed 'nooks and crannies'. There are 'obvious' places for these, like next to the front door or in front of the living room windows, where they are easily seen from indoors, but it is a good idea to position some of your plantings further away so that you are enticed out into the garden to see them properly. Having succumbed to curiosity, you will then be drawn on by another interesting piece of planting just round the next bend, and another beyond it half hidden behind a small group of shrubs. . . . It is important to build this element of curiosity into any garden, but especially into a small one which could otherwise be viewed at a glance in its entirety, without going out into it at all.

Many of the most successful larger cottage gardens have taken this idea of grouping plants together into distinct seasonal corners one step further by creating a series of 'gardens within a garden' – areas with completely different personalities linked by paths, paving or lawn. Some of these miniature gardens will be planned as spring features, while others, intended to look their best at different times of year, lie dormant in spring,

In this pocket-handkerchief-sized London garden, the element of curiosity has been very successfully introduced simply by planting a block of camellias to obscure the direct view down the garden, and allowing the path to wind out of sight round the corner, teasing the onlooker to discover what lies beyond.

The pond at Cameo Cottage, Essex; this part of the garden is naturally damp, so water features such as this and the nearby wellhead were an obvious choice to exploit the existing potential of the site. In the foreground is part of a craggy rockscape which has been created by forming the basic shape with scrunched-up wire netting, covering it with hypertufa (peat, sand and cement) and allowing it to weather. Pockets of gritty soil have been planted with choice rock plants, aubrieta and 'Goldheart' ivy. The stepping stones over the pond are also artificial, being supported on submerged oil drums placed wherever the owners felt a crossing was needed – a very necessary arrangement as the pond is a large one surrounded by extensive planting. Early colour round the margins is provided by *Trollius* and drumstick primulas.

or appear as a green area of foliage. Others again may depend for their character on additional elements, such as containers and paving, and may be planted up to provide a range of seasonal interest.

Gardens within a Garden

At Cameo Cottage in Essex, for instance, the garden contains several separate 'gardens', each with its own special character, yet with no formal barriers between them. (These are in fact the 'cameos' that give the cottage its name). The individual nature of each is created by varying the plants, and by the different hard features used, such as containers, rockery, walling or garden furniture, and also by the surface underfoot, which changes – from lawn to gravel to stone flags to grass paths between borders and even to wooden bridges – as you slowly progress from one 'garden' to the next.

At the front door of the cottage is a small paved area, nicknamed by the

owner 'Matilda's garden' after a small stone statue of a girl half hidden by plants near the hedge. Matilda's garden is dominated by a gnarled old crab apple tree and a huge *Magnolia stellata*, in the shade of which grow a profusion of bluebells, *Helleborus corsicus*, *Euphorbia cyparissias*, and tiny creeping plants, filling the cracks between the stones and forming the backdrop to a jumble of containers crammed with small alpine 'treasures'.

Across the lawn is another 'cameo'; a striking feature made from what appears to be the foot of an old spiral staircase. This was built using bricks from an old post office that was demolished many years ago in the village, to provide height to an otherwise flat corner of the garden. Now, a sunken path paved with old tiles winds round the base of the 'stairway', which is actually a large brick-sided raised bed with a second raised bed built in part of it to give a two-storey stepped effect. Large sprawling old plants of *Erysimum* 'Bowles' Mauve' provide much of the spring colour here, though this is not primarily a spring feature. Just visible behind the stairway, is a secret corner with an old seat in the shade of a densely planted group of spring-flowering *Viburnum* × *bodnantense* 'Dawn', a red-flowered witch hazel and a blue cedar. The whole area is underplanted with winter aconites and snowdrops, and though the effect is distinctly overcrowded, it gives the illusion that the plants grew there naturally – a very effective cottage gardener's ploy.

Further on, in a damp, slightly shaded area, is another spring 'cameo' where both the purple and white forms of the snakeshead fritillary (*Fritillaria meleagris*) have seeded themselves between cracks in paving and in the borders, and their nodding, chequered flowers create a stunning though short-lived display, together with early-flowering primulas and wood anemones. Nearby is the pond backed by an impressive – and entirely artificial – craggy rock grotto. This is made from hypertufa, a mixture of sand, cement and peat, 'weathered' by a few drenches of dilute cow manure to encourage the growth of lichens and mosses. It contains several planting pockets filled with gritty soil for rock plants, while on the banks of the pond are drifts of candelabra and drumstick primulas, which flower in late spring. Crossing the pond, which is a large one, are a series of stepping stones supported unromantically but very practically on the tops of submerged oil drums. Still in the damp part of the garden, is a reconstructed wellhead, planted in shades of yellow – *Alyssum saxatile* grows in its walls, double celandines round the base, and the surrounding paving supports thriving colonies of yellow-flowered *Sisyrinchium* and lady's mantle. A dwarf willow, *Salix lanata*, grows nearby in a hypertufa container.

A disused agricultural ditch runs right across the middle of the garden. This never dries right out even in midsummer, and has been planted with a tremendous selection of bog-garden plants, and moisture and shade lovers,

Waterside planting at Cameo Cottage, with flowering saxifrage on the raised rock feature overhanging marsh marigold (*Caltha palustris*) at the water's edge.

including foxgloves, primulas, double primroses and violets. The ditch is crossed here and there by rustic bridges which are functional as well as ornamental; every time the owner needed a place to take a wheelbarrow across, a bridge was built and now the walk round the garden involves several crossings, each one taking you into a new 'cameo' beyond.

In the furthest corner of the garden, a particularly shady and quiet one, a brick archway leads through to a cool and secluded 'cameo' of greens and whites, hidden away within a tiny walled garden paved with matching old bricks. Like a lot of successful green and white gardens, this one looks

The ornamental wellhead at Cameo Cottage is planted with yellow flowers for a spring display. Here, double celandines (*Ranunculus ficaria* 'Flore Pleno') are combined with *Alyssum saxatile* and the fluffy catkins of *Salix lanata*, which grows in a nearby tub.

The wellhead has been built with a double outer wall which, filled with soil, now provides planting places for a range of spring flowers. Although the colour scheme is predominately yellow, small touches of other colours have crept in, in the form of aubrieta, marigolds and the odd self-seeded fritillary.

deceptively simple but relies on two very deliberate design elements for its success. One is the selection of plants for the texture and form of their foliage – there is the widest possible mixture of matt and shiny leaves, linear and rounded leaves, upright and bushy plant shapes. The other is the way the very merest hint of another colour – in this case mauve – has been introduced among the greens and whites to give shading and depth to the scheme. In spring, the basic colour scheme is provided by white-flowered forms of thyme, foreget-me-not, Jacob's ladder, *Anthemis*, *Tradescantia*, aquilegia, *Campanula*, *Leucojum*, bluebells, viola, ivy-leaved toadflax, *Ornith-ogalum* and *Cyclamen*, interspersed with the green flowers of *Euphorbia amygdaloides robbiae*, *Alchemilla mollis*, woodruff, fern foliage and the catkins of *Garrya elliptica*. The vital touch of mauve is provided by campanulas that have seeded themselves shadow-like among the other plants.

From the cool quiet of the green and white garden, the path turns abruptly round a corner into bright sunlight and the top end of the ditch, over which a wooden bridge leads into a garden of strong architectural shapes, dominated by massive clumps of self-sown *Euphorbia characias wulfenii*. Winding gravel paths twist their way between tall tree trunks laden with *Clematis alpina*, *Euphorbia characias wulfenii* 'Lambrook Gold' (a golden-flowered form) and several spectacular mature specimens of golden-flowered *Paeonia mlokosewitschii*, until reaching the back of the house where a bed of asphodels, aquilegias, forget-me-nots and bluebells framed against the magnolia and crab apple of Matilda's garden provides the link back into the paved area by the front door.

Although the overall effect of the garden – which is quite large as cottage gardens go – is of a total spring garden, it is only because the effect of each 'cameo' is strong enough to distract your attention from the areas where there is no spring interest. The garden looks completely different as the season progresses and the cameos change through summer and autumn.

The Use of Key Plants

A larger cottage garden still is that of the late Margery Fish (the well-known author of many books on gardening including *Cottage Garden Flowers*), whose garden at East Lambrook Manor, South Petherton in Somerset, is still maintained by the current owners very much as she planted it. Again there are a series of linked 'gardens', but here the individual gardens are larger and tend to run into each other. A particularly noticeable feature of the design is that, although each area has its own separate personality, certain 'key plants' have been used through-out the garden to give a feeling of continuity. *Euphorbia characias wulfenii*, a late-spring flower, crops up everywhere, but features particularly extens-ively in a densely planted area of *Euphorbia*, carpeting plants and trimmed, man-sized yew trees, close to the house. This 'garden' is almost like a maze being full of narrow winding paths that double back on themselves so that, with the view restricted by rounded yews, you cannot be certain which way you are facing.

Another spring flower that is the star of its own special area but which crops up in a minor role throughout the garden, is *Brunnera macrophylla*. With large kidney-shaped leaves and long, lax spikes of forget-me-not flowers, this forms an important part of the planting in one of the two large ditches which are a particular feature of Margery Fish's garden. The less shady of the two is carpeted entirely with low ground-covering, moisture-loving plants which grow between the *Brunnera* – primroses, bluebells, cranesbill, violets and double celandines – through which you can walk with difficulty on slippery stepping stones that are almost hidden by foliage. The *Brunnera* recurs regularly as ground cover beneath shrubs in both sunny and shady spots – the plant is at home almost anywhere.

Pollarded willows are a feature of this very natural-looking damp shady area at East Lambrook Manor, Somerset. The carpet of plants beneath shows the marvellous patterns that can be created by combining a variety of plant and foliage shapes, sizes and textures.

Shapes play an important part in the garden at
East Lambrook Manor. In this area, close to the
house, trimmed yew trees are dotted among
carpets of smaller plants – perennial candytuft,
wallflowers, primroses, *Bergenia*, *Brunnera* –
interwoven with a maze of narrow winding
paths. Here, the focus is firmly kept on close
detail, but eventually the path leads out to a
different sort of planting framing a long distant
view.

Large blocks of solid planting are a recurrent
feature at East Lambrook Manor. *Euphorbia
characias wulfenii* occurs repeatedly throughout
the garden, besides appearing as the main
spring feature in one or two of the 'gardens
within a garden'.

Aquilegia (granny's bonnets) is a traditional old cottage-garden plant that should be included in any scheme. It looks good grown among other spring-flowering plants and shrubs, or against a background of foliage (perhaps that of plants for flowering later in summer), and is specially useful in adding height to a spring display. Named varieties of aquilegia are available in a good range of colours, but the traditional old cottage-garden favourite has blue flowers. Once established, plants will seed themselves freely, but aquilegias are notorious for the freedom with which they cross-pollinate, so do not be surprised if the resulting seedlings are not always the same colour as the parent. Do, however, allow at least a few seedlings to remain where they appear in odd corners and crevices – they help create a misty romantic feel to the garden, without making any work!

As you walk round Margery Fish's garden the picture alternates between close detail and distant views. From the area near the house where your view is restricted by solid evergreens to the plants just in front of you, you move on to another 'garden' where your eye is led by a long straight path through low carpet planting to a landscape of lovely old outbuildings, prettily framed by a large flat-topped golden-leaved tree and neatly clipped dome-shaped yew. Yet at every stage of your tour, you cannot help but be aware that if you turn round you are confronted by a completely different view.

Adapting Ideas to a Small Garden

The idea of creating different views is particularly applicable to a large garden. Yet even in a small cottage garden, it is still possible to do so to some extent simply by varying the height of adjacent plantings, and by concentrating groupings of larger shrubs to act as barriers between individual 'gardens' of small plants. It is also possible in a small space to establish different identities for separate groups of plants simply by choosing species that have something in common, such as shade tolerance, or those suitable for waterside planting, and providing them with suitable surroundings – an old stone container for bulbs, a patch of stone flags for alpine plants, a small pond or bog garden for waterside plants, or an interesting tree or group of trees to shelter shade lovers.

It is a good idea to visit a number of other cottage gardens when hunting out ideas to incorporate in your own; and even if you have only a very tiny garden, do not be put off visiting larger ones, particularly if they are designed on this 'gardens within a garden' principal – you'll often find that any one individual 'cameo' could make a very nice small cottage garden in its own right.

As a general rule, this 'gardens within a garden' style of planting will need very much more care and attention than the original cottage gardens. Of necessity, the early cottagers' gardens had to be easy to maintain, and they would have had a very practical no-nonsense design. The space at the back of the house would probably have been largely devoted to vegetables, while the front garden contained most of the colour and interest. Here there may have been several large old apple trees casting light dappled shade over a wall-to-wall border filled with a solid carpet of narcissi, primroses and primulas, leaving just enough room for a straight path running through it from the garden gate to the front door of the house. As spring progressed, the subsiding daffodil foliage would have been overtaken by rampant ground-covering plants such as bluebells, comfrey and *Pulmonaria*, punctuated by crown imperials, clumps of hellebores, lily-of-the-valley, violets or whatever else the cottager had thought fit to naturalize in the semi-shade. Near the path, where the shade would have

Hellebores are a favourite flower in cottage gardens. *H. orientalis* flowers in late winter and early spring. It is very variable, with flowers from pink to wine red and often attractively spotted, and makes a colourful addition to the spring garden. In a good position it will propagate itself from naturally shed seed and produce an interesting mixture of shades.

Flowering cherry is perhaps one of the shortest lasting of the spring blossoms, but one of the prettiest. Even the fallen petals look good scattered over the lawn. Many cultivars of the popular Japanese cherries have bronze-tinted new foliage which contrasts most effectively with the shell pink of the flowers.

been lighter and the plants more disciplined, a more formal style of planting was often used with rows of intermingled wallflowers and cottage tulips backing smaller edging plants such as auriculas or double daisies. Against the wall of the house would have grown winter jasmine or *Chaenomeles*, the ornamental quince.

Nowadays, with a much wider range of plants available to us, a garden of this type, whether at the front or back of the house, provides an ideal environment for growing spring-flowering woodland plants such as trilliums, dog's tooth violets and Solomon's seal, as well as other plants that thrive in semi-shade like *Euphorbia amygdaloides robbiae*, *Brunnera*, double *Ranunculus ficaria*, old named varieties of violas, primroses and double-flowered lady's smock. Spring bulbs are a good choice too, since they flower and complete their growth cycle early enough in the year not to be bothered by shade later on in the season; you can quite safely plant snowdrops, winter aconites, miniature narcissi and hardy cyclamen. The old apple trees, if they still exist, are more often decorative than useful now, and serve as rustic supports for clematis or honeysuckle, which ramble attractively up through the branches. In a sunny spot, old sinks or troughs of encrusted saxifrages and miniature bulbs make a good focal point, and 'special' corners could be used for treasures like the old double wallflowers 'Harpur Crewe' and 'Bloody Warrior', or the variegated crown imperial.

Where space is short, be sure to include a lot of small spring-flowering plants rather than a few larger ones. Spring-flowering plants normally have a much shorter season than summer ones, and if you are to maintain a display it is important to include many different species so that as one goes over there is always something new to take its place. In a small garden that relies mainly on its summer display, a good spring show can be achieved by using 'temporary' plants – wallflowers, polyanthus, forget-me-nots and primroses bedded out in the early autumn after summer annuals have been cleared, or pots of spring bulbs plunged into position after the foliage is well grown or the flower buds are beginning to open. Spring-flowering bulbs can also be planted out in the autumn and then lifted after the flowers are over and heeled into a quiet corner of the vegetable garden until the foliage dies down, leaving room for summer annuals or herbaceous plants to follow on in their place. And in even the tiniest spaces – literally a small pocket of soil at the bottom of a hedge or wall – there is always room for a selection of the smaller spring-flowering plants, such as the various forms of bugle (well worth growing for their pretty, crinkly purple or red foliage, which smothers weeds), *Primula rosea*, lady's smock and the double form of it, double celandines, *Arabis*, auriculas or aubrieta. No matter how small the space, a splash of colour at the end of a long cold dark winter enlivens the garden and lifts the spirits.

Even in a wild garden it is possible to introduce a colour scheme very effectively. Here the yellow of daffodils, newly opened willow shoots and naturally occurring mossy hillocks contrast pleasingly with drifts of purple primroses.

2

An Abundance of Roses

Roses and cottages are synonymous; who could imagine a picturesque old-world cottage without its roses round the door? The nostalgic association between cottages and roses extends to real life too; roses are probably the single most popular garden flower. They have everything – good looks, a wide range of culinary, medicinal, cosmetic and decorative uses, and a long and romantic history.

A gate in the wall leads from one part of this Oxfordshire garden to another, and the roses form a perfect frame for what lies beyond.

Lots of roses give the illusion of being old fashioned, but are actually of comparatively recent breeding. This is 'Nevada' (1927), one of the most popular modern shrub roses ever to have been produced. The flowers are large – about 4 in (10 cm) across, creamy coloured with golden yellow stamens – and plentifully produced. In early summer, the plants are completely smothered with bloom.

A particularly old group of the genuinely old roses are the Damasks, which are thought to have been brought back from the Crusades by returning noblemen. 'Ispahan' (also known as 'Pompom des Princes') has a longer flowering season than most Damask roses, and is exceptionally highly perfumed.

The roses from which most old garden roses developed are thought to have originated in the Middle East in the area around Persia, and were gradually spread round the world by early colonists. As a result of centuries of crossbreeding, the original rose species have been translated into a huge range of varieties with many different characteristics. And many more arrive on the scene each year, as breeders constantly vie with each other to bring out something new. Nowadays, roses come in all shapes and sizes, ranging from huge climbers and ramblers to bushes and neatly trained standards, to the prostrate ground-covering kinds and tiny miniatures. They include every colour except black; you can even find roses with green, almost blue, brown and grey flowers. Many varieties are exceptionally heavily perfumed, while others are grown primarily for their hips or occasionally for their foliage.

Types of Roses

From the cottage gardener's point of view, roses can be divided into four main types – modern bush roses, old-fashioned roses, Climbing and Rambler roses, and species roses. Modern Hybrid Teas flower continuously from early summer to the first autumn frosts. Although they are sometimes grown as long-flowering shrubs in cottage gardens, they are generally considered too 'modern' for this style of garden.

OLD-FASHIONED ROSES

Old-fashioned roses are the favourites for cottage gardens. As the name suggests, they are much earlier roses; some varieties still grown date back as far as the sixteenth century. It's not just their age that makes old-fashioned roses so interesting, their flowers are quite a different shape to those of Hybrid Teas. Many varieties have much flatter flowers, while others have 'quartered', pompon-shaped or striped blooms; Moss roses are so called because of the green moss-like glands covering the buds and tips of the young shoots. Old-fashioned roses are also in general more highly scented than modern Hybrid Teas, many of which have no scent at all. Neither do they need the hard annual pruning required to keep Hybrid Tea roses looking their best. Old-fashioned roses should be pruned like normal shrubs; just enough to tidy them up if and when they need it. But charming though they undoubtedly are, the drawback to most old roses is their short flowering period. Many kinds will only produce one flush of blooms in early summer, and nothing else for the rest of the year. Some have a second short burst in early autumn, while others, after their main flush in early summer, continue flowering spasmodically throughout much of the same season as Hybrid Teas. Despite this apparent drawback, many cottage gardeners grow old-fashioned roses in preference to Hybrid Teas as they are more in keeping with the period of an old cottage.

Many of the old-fashioned roses have tall, rather lax stems which are easier to manage, as well as tidier to look at, when supported in some way. Here a rose is trained over an arch of rustic poles; 'wings' at the sides contain wayward stems and help make it a more substantial-looking feature.

Most roses were developed as a result of deliberate breeding but this one, named 'Betty Hussey', was discovered in 1977 growing in a field in Berkshire, probably as a result of a chance seed dropped by a bird. It is now growing at an Old Rectory nearby. The owners exhibited it at a Royal Horticultural Society show in 1987, where it received an Award of Merit. At the time of writing it is only available from one small nursery in Surrey. 'Betty Hussey' is a large vigorous climber of the same sort of habit and growth as the giant 'Kiftsgate' – so you need plenty of room if you want to try it!

The name 'old-fashioned rose' covers a very wide range of varieties, which are divided into several different 'families' based on their original parentage. There are Albas, Gallicas, Rugosas, Moss roses, Centifolias or cabbage roses, Sweet Briars, and so on, all of which contain a number of named varieties sharing particular characteristics such as flowering season, scent, prickliness, hardiness, or the ability to produce a good crop of hips. So when choosing old roses, it's worth picking from several different 'families' to get a good cross section of types. The Alba group (which includes 'Maiden's Blush') are very hardy plants tolerant of poor conditions, with upright stems and few spines, but flowering only in midsummer. Damask roses (including 'Blush Damask' and 'Madame Hardy') are rather weak floppy plants with well-scented flowers in midsummer followed by slim, bristly hips. Gallicas include a lot of popular

'Fru Dagmar Hastrup' is a Rugosa rose which makes a good but comparatively compact bush. Plants grow to about 5 ft (1.5 m) high, and flower repeatedly throughout the summer, producing a reliable crop of large round red fruit which is often ripening at the same time as the last flush of flowers open. Like most Rugosas, this variety is tolerant of a wide range of conditions and having very prickly stems, makes a wind-resistant and stock-proof hedge.

varieties such as 'Cardinal de Richelieu', 'Charles de Mills', 'Tuscany', the old apothecary's rose (*R. gallica officinalis*) and the striped rosa mundi (otherwise known as *R. gallica* 'Versicolor'); they are highly scented and will put up with poor soil, but flower only in midsummer. Dwarf Polyanthas (such as 'Cécile Brunner') have lots of small flowers in midsummer with a few more in early autumn. Hybrid Musks are more modern than some old-fashioned roses; they include popular varieties like 'Ballerina' and 'Buff Beauty', all of which start flowering in midsummer and continue into the autumn. Rugosas are very tough, wind-tolerant roses with prickly stems well suited to being grown as flowering hedges or shelter belts; they flower intermittently from midsummer to autumn, when the last flowers often coincide with the heavy crop of hips. Popular Rugosa roses include 'Pink Grootendorst', 'Fru Dagmar Hastrup' and 'Roseraie de l'Haÿ' (which does not have hips). Moss roses, with their sticky green or occasionally brown moss-like growth round buds and new shoots, are all derived from sports of the cabbage rose, *R. × centifolia*. The flowers, which are produced only in midsummer, are highly perfumed, and the 'moss' also contributes a slightly resinous scent when bruised. Well-known varieties include 'William Lobb', Old Pink Moss, and 'Blanche Moreau'. Bourbon roses are another 'family' with many popular offspring such as 'Madame Isaac Pereire', 'Souvenir de la Malmaison', 'Zéphirine Drouhin' and the striped 'Variegata di Bologna'. They are vigorous plants, among the most popular of shrub roses, with good reason, as they flower from early summer intermittently through till the autumn frosts. There are a few other 'families' but those mentioned include most of the best-known.

The short or intermittent flowering period of many old-fashioned roses need not be a great disadvantage to the cottage gardener, as it provides plenty of opportunities for varying the look of the garden by underplanting with other summer flowers – something that is very difficult to do attractively with non-stop-flowering Hybrid Tea roses. However, for the person wanting the best of both worlds, the rose breeder David Austin is now producing 'English Roses', which combine the appearance of old-fashioned roses with the continuous flowering of Hybrid Teas.

CLIMBING ROSES AND RAMBLERS
Climbing roses and Ramblers have not attracted quite so much attention from breeders as the more popular bush roses, and virtually any of them are perfectly 'in keeping' as cottage-garden plants. Some of the larger old-fashioned roses, too, have a sufficiently lax habit of growth to make them suitable for training either as large bushes or as climbers. Both Climbers and Ramblers can be trained through trees, up rustic poles to give height to a border, over screens, trellis, outbuildings, walls and fences. Being less highly bred than Hybrid Teas, Climbers and Ramblers have similar

The climbing rose 'New Dawn' is not too rampant so is suitable for growing through a small tree as seen in this small orchard. It is not a particularly old variety – it was bred in 1930 – but the silvery pink, flowers are beautifully scented.

Rosa sericea pteracantha is grown entirely for its huge flat translucent red spines, and is best seen with the light behind it.

flowering tendencies to shrub roses, and concentrate their flowering in midsummer. Some varieties will however flower again in the autumn, while others flower on and off throughout the summer.

SPECIES ROSES

Species roses and their immediate hybrids tend to be rather large plants suitable as specimens in larger gardens, but often used as robust, stock-proof, flowering hedges in cottage gardens. Some are good for wild corners, and being more robust than the more highly bred kinds, species roses are usually the best choice for difficult situations – poor soil, windswept sites, etc. The flowers of species roses are, in general, much less spectacular than those of the other groups, but this is compensated for by their brilliant autumn display of colourful hips, which is what they are mainly grown for. Some species roses have other interesting features, such as the enormous translucent flat red spines of *Rosa sericea pteracantha*. *Rosa glauca* (synonym *R. rubrifolia*) has pretty silvery mauve foliage much appreciated by flower arrangers, while *Rosa eglanteria*, the sweet briar or eglantine, has aromatic foliage producing an apple-like scent, especially after rain.

Using Roses in Cottage Gardens

Cottage gardeners of the past would clearly have had a very much more restricted choice of roses than that available to us today. The true

In this cottage garden in Buckinghamshire, a solidly planted rose bed has a path of broken tiles which allows you to pick your way through. The roses are interplanted with herbaceous plants to make a contrast in shape and colour, and to prolong the interest when old-fashioned varieties are not in bloom.

At Duncombe Farm, Hertfordshire, the garden is virtually solid plants punctuated by paths – there is no lawn. Here, shrub roses provide islands of height and colourful centrepieces to areas circumnavigated by winding paths, and are a leafy backdrop to herbaceous flowers and low shrubs when not in flower.

The mixture of different climbers on the front wall of Peartwater Cottage, Somerset, reflects the extravagant planting of the surrounding garden. Climbing roses are teamed with *Pyracantha* and several different varieties of clematis to provide a long season of interest.

cottagers, not being able to buy plants for the garden, would probably have had the dog rose, sweet briar and other naturalized species growing wild in their hedgerows. They would also have acquired cuttings of such shrub (old-fashioned) roses as were available at the time, and which found their way from the gardens of large houses. (Shrub roses root easily from cuttings). The older roses such as 'Maiden's Blush', York and Lancaster, cabbage roses and Moss roses would have been likely candidates. Occasionally, roses would have 'arrived' as seed dropped by birds, and been left to grow.

In old cottage gardens, roses were grown as bushes in the border, against a wall or over a porch or a bower (an arch of rustic poles over a seat, the roof and back clad with climbing plants). But I think it is probably true to say that we make very much more use of roses in modern cottage gardens. Roses are so popular now, and there are so many more different kinds cheaply and easily available; also our gardens are more planned and structured, so we find more places to put them.

Cottage gardens today rarely have a formal rose garden of Hybrid Teas. Modern cottage gardeners – like their predecessors – prefer to grow the species and old-fashioned shrub roses. Because these roses generally have a relatively short flowering season, they are not grown separately but like any other flowering shrub are placed in mixed borders to add height, variety, and scent to a collection of different cottage-garden plants. Often they are used in graduated planting towards the back of a border or in the centre of a bed that can be seen from all sides. They are generally underplanted with low spreading subjects such as hardy geraniums, phlox, campanula, lavender, *Alchemilla mollis*, *Astrantia* and spring bulbs, with groups of taller plants such as delphiniums and *Eryngium* pushing their way up between them. At Duncombe Farm, in Hertfordshire, for instance, where the garden consists of 'wall-to-wall' planting with paths winding through it, shrub roses provide height at the back of the wide borders and in the centre of 'island' planting. At one side of the garden, roses are used in a gentle build up of height to the old orchard beyond, and make a natural barrier between the two very different styles of garden and orchard.

Climbing and Rambler roses are also used in modern cottage gardens to cover arches, walls and fences. These roses associate well with other kinds of climbers, such as honeysuckle, *Pyracantha* or clematis, or a mixture of several climbers can be grown together as they are on the walls of Peartwater Cottage, Somerset. But clematis is probably the most popular climber to mix with climbing roses. By choosing a very early-flowering clematis such as *C. cirrhosa*, its form *C.c. balearica*, or in a suitably sheltered spot, *C. armandii*, and a summer-flowering one with a long season such as *C. × jackmanii*, it is possible to have continuously floriferous walls almost all the year round, although the climbing rose will only be in flower for part of

Shrub and species roses are often used as hedges, but here is an alternative way of making a natural-looking barrier. At Field Farm, Kent, they have created an informal screen of roses which separates the cottage garden from the surrounding fields, and also offers much needed protection from the strong winds in what is otherwise a very exposed site.

that time. Similarly, when climbing and rambling roses are grown up through trees, by dovetailing the flowering time of the 'host' tree and climbing rose you can achieve double the value from a small space. You can prolong the flowering season further still and give even more variety to the garden by adding a clematis to the collection.

Old-fashioned roses, which are often tall and lax in growth, adapt well to being grown on all kinds of structures, too. Supported by rustic poles, as at Watermeadows, in Somerset they can help add height to an otherwise rather flat-looking border. Often gardeners grow roses and other climbers on a lattice-like structure of poles to form a raised background to a border, or to screen out an uninteresting view. This is a particularly useful way of growing weak-stemmed roses, and is a most attractive and practical way of dealing with them. Large species and old-fashioned roses can also be usefully employed as hedges, windbreaks or screens, as well as grown in borders for purely decorative effect. At Field Farm, Kent, an informal screen of roses and other large shrubs separates the cottage garden

At Watermeadows, Somerset, besides growing shrub roses in the border, climbers are used to introduce a variation in height to an otherwise flat garden. Here, they are growing up a framework of rustic poles lining a walk, and are also trained up tall upright stakes. Besides looking good and making the best possible use of space, these growing methods make it very easy to keep the roses under control.

bordering the house from the surrounding fields, besides providing some shelter for the more precious plants within – a necessary requirement for a garden in a very exposed situation.

An Informal Rose Garden

Rose enthusiasts sometimes set aside a particular area as a rose garden, concentrating a collection of their favourite varieties in one spot. Here, roses take pride of place over other trees and shrubs – though there will be other smaller flowers chosen to complement the roses and to act in a supporting role after the peak of the rose season is over. The front garden of a fifteenth-century cottage at Ditchling, in East Sussex, is a good example. Here, the owner has created a rose garden that not only houses her favourite varieties, but that also provides continuity of colour and interest throughout most of the year by using a well-chosen blend of ground-covering plants beneath the roses. The result is very successful. Although the space is no bigger than most small front gardens, twenty-five different

Roses are inseparable from cottages. The traditional place to grow them is round the door, but in most cottage gardens you will also find old-fashioned roses grown as flowering shrubs in mixed borders, and Climbers or Ramblers on walls and trained over arches. And given the tremendous range of cultivars available, it is not unusual to find that enthusiasts will often use their rose collection to form the backbone of a special part of the garden, filling in under the bushes with a mixture of low ground-hugging cottage garden plants to prolong the flowering season. The result automatically has an attractively old-world cottage garden ambience about it.

varieties of rose and several other shrubs and climbing plants grow there in delightful profusion, underplanted with a mixture of chalk-tolerant ground-covering plants (the garden is on slightly alkaline soil).

From the garden gate, you walk down an old brick path flanked by wide borders towards the front door of the cottage, which is clad in a mass of winter jasmine. To the right of the front door a large tree of *Abutilon vitifolium* supports a rare old double clematis, *C. viticella* 'Purpurea Plena Elegans', whose small double faded-lavender flowers are set off beautifully by the grey felty leaves of the *Abutilon* in midsummer.

A large L-shaped border fills the centre of the front garden. All round the edge of the plot is another wide border, leaving a grass path between just wide enough to negotiate a way through the roses. In such a small space the owner has wisely decided to keep the planting of all the main beds to a constant theme. Roses form the chief attraction except in the narrow beds beneath the cottage windows, which are planted solely with low-growing plants such as lavender – roses here would obscure the view. A very striking tall hedge of purple-leaved *Prunus cerasifera* 'Pissardii' borders the street. When viewed from the house, this makes a most effective backdrop for the rose garden.

The layout of the garden is very informal; the owner allowed it to 'grow' as her interest in old-fashioned roses grew, in much the same way as the original cottage gardens 'happened'. Whenever she wanted to add new plants, she simply widened her borders until now all that remains of the lawn is a series of grass paths of varying width, and a small patch of grass under a particularly large specimen rose bush. The general effect is very natural, the garden looks delightfully untouched and rambling, and gives the impression of being 'undiscovered'.

But for all its charmingly natural planting scheme, the garden is in fact much planned when it comes to the plants that have been chosen, in order

When you walk round the garden at Ditchling in early summer, the impression is of solid roses. However, it was never designed to be so. Originally, narrow beds were made on either side of the brick path and along the front of the garden, but when the owner became fascinated by old-fashioned roses and began to collect them, the beds were expanded until now very little of the old lawn remains.

to achieve a long flowering season. With this in mind, quite a few repeat-flowering roses have been used, though not exclusively. Under the roses, the ground is completely filled with low-growing, spreading plants chosen to flower in succession from early spring to autumn. The garden year begins with spring bulbs, hellebores, primulas and iris. The roses follow on, with many varieties continuing to flower spasmodically through the summer above a random patchwork of pinks, erodiums, hardy geraniums, lavender, *Cistus*, *Potentilla*, *Campanula*, *Sisyrinchium* and *Veronica*. In autumn, some of the roses will put on a second, late show of flowers, while others provide a good crop of hips, complemented by Michaelmas daisies, nerines, *Schizostylis* and *Clematis rehderiana*. After leaf-fall, stems of dogwood provide a late splash of colour.

3

The Garden Harvest

Fruit and vegetables were, once upon a time, the most important plants to be found in a cottage garden. The cottagers of centuries ago depended on their gardens for much of their food – fruit, vegetables, and honey – as well as for herbs for medicinal and cosmetic use and a wide variety of other household purposes. But as times became more affluent, cottage gardens became more ornamental. Fortunately, there is now a resurgence of interest in some of the old ways of growing fruit and vegetables, and many 'antique' varieties are once again becoming available.

There is nothing quite like harvesting your own crops to give you the true flavour of a good, old-fashioned cottage garden. This is pleasantly followed by the sense of achievement that comes when you serve guests with your own home-grown fruit, vegetables and preserves. Growing your own enables you to produce a much more interesting range of varieties than you could buy in the shops; they'll be fresher, too, and you can be certain they have been grown without artificial fertilizers and pesticides.

Adding a hint of the old 'cottage economy' to the garden is very evocative, and it gives a great feeling of satisfaction to be able to fill a freezer with your own produce, serve up fresh, homegrown crops, or display home-made preserves on the kitchen dresser. Growing your own is also a good idea if you want to be certain of having fruit and vegetables free from synthetic chemicals, or if you want to be able to eat a wide range of unusual crops not generally available in the shops.

Planted with thought and care, vegetables and fruit can be a most attractive addition to the garden, helping to extend the cottage-garden year with spring blossom, colourful foliage and a variety of interesting leaf shapes, colours and textures throughout the summer, followed by beautifully coloured autumn fruits.

Early Cottage Gardens

If you go back to the beginning of civilized cottage society, around the twelfth century, herbs, vegetables and fruit were largely grown in monastery gardens. It is most likely that the early cottagers – agricultural peasants – got their plants from the monks. The range of crops available would have been rather restricted. Some plants, notably fruit trees, had already been brought into Britain by the Romans and other invaders – the old costard apple, a large rather coarse fruit, has been grown in cottage gardens since earliest times. Others were derived by cultivating native species and selecting the best forms. From the evidence available, the most commonly grown crops in the early days of cottage life were those that could be stored for winter use, like onions, garlic and shallots, leeks, carrots, turnips, skirret (rather like a parsnip) and beet. Winter kale was hardy enough to withstand a winter in the open. Salad crops and green vegetables such as lettuce, orache, cabbage and sorrel were also cultivated, and were valuable sources of vitamins in early spring after a long winter on a limited diet. Wild 'greens', such as watercress, dandelion leaves, and corn salad were picked from the countryside. Peas and beans were both grown to use fresh or dried for winter.

The staple diet of cottagers at this time was pottage, a savoury cereal porridge flavoured with whatever meat, herbs and vegetables were available. Sometimes the winter pottage was based on peas; this was the original 'pease pottage'.

Wild raspberries, strawberries, elderberries and hazelnuts were available in the countryside by way of a seasonal treat. But since fresh fruit was thought to be dangerous (the effects of eating too much of it are similar to fever symptoms), it was usually cooked and eaten as a sort of fruit version of pottage.

As time passed by, many of the fruits and vegetables we now regard as ordinary garden plants were gradually introduced from other countries.

The essential touch for an authentic-looking fruit and vegetable plot in the country.

Vegetable gardens need not be an untidy mess, to be hidden away out of sight. Well tended and attractively laid out, they can be valuable features in a garden, bringing a touch of orderliness that creates an interesting contrast to the informality of the flower borders. This traditional vegetable plot in Berkshire is a small garden in its own right – a neat arrangement of different shapes, textures and colours.

Brussels sprouts were not cultivated in Britain until the 1600s, and potatoes were not commonly grown except by the Irish until late in the seventeenth century. It was not until the eighteenth century that a wider selection of the more easily propagated fruit trees and bushes began to be cultivated in cottage gardens. By now the staple food of the cottager had changed to bread and cheese, although pottage was still eaten for breakfast and supper. (The tradition of porridge for breakfast continues to this day in Scotland.) So despite the fact that a much more varied and interesting range of foodstuffs would have been available to the wealthy classes, the cottagers' daily fare was distinctly dull, plain and repetitious until as recently as the last century – enlivened only by what they could grow for themselves in the garden.

Incorporating Fruit and Vegetables in a Cottage Garden

In the early days of cottage gardening, vegetables and other useful crops such as herbs must have occupied the whole garden. As centuries went by,

these would have been joined by flowering plants like primroses and wild geraniums dug up from the surrounding countryside, until eventually, with acquisitions from the grounds of large houses, cottage gardens contained a mixture of edible and ornamental plants. To begin with, flowers and vegetables would have been planted pretty much at random wherever there was space. But as cottage gardens became more sophisticated, in the last couple of centuries, practical and ornamental gardening were gradually separated. Back gardens became the place to grow fruit and vegetables, while front gardens were reserved for flowers. Modern

A neat, well-planned and well-kept vegetable plot is just as interesting to walk round as a flowerbed – with the bonus of good things to come later. This back garden in Surrey is entirely planted with fruit and vegetables, which are grown very intensively. Cloches help bring on early crops in the spring as well as prolonging the growing season in autumn. And in country areas, a fruit cage is the safest way of keeping birds away from the fruit.

At Watermeadows, Somerset, the garden is divided up by grass paths, and the vegetables are grown at the pointed end of a long narrow triangular plot. There are roses and flowers at the end nearest the house, and the occasional pillar of Rambler roses along the edge to help camouflage the vegetables. At the furthest tip of the triangle are the compost heaps, which provide a constant supply of organic material for use all round the garden.

gardeners have often phased out edible crops entirely to make more space for ornamental plantings. However, fruit and vegetables can be incorporated into a cottage garden in ways that are both ornamental and traditional. And though some of the planting styles may be 'borrowed' from the big house rather than the peasant's cottage, they nevertheless look very much 'at home' in cottage gardens.

THE VEGETABLE PLOT

One way to incorporate fruit and vegetables into a cottage garden is to set aside a specific plot. But instead of giving them a separate bed in the conventional manner, plant them behind the flowers at the back of a border, or even in the middle of a large bed with flowers and flowering shrubs growing around the edges. In this way, you catch glimpses of the vegetables through the flowers, and they provide an interesting background of foliage. This simple technique creates a delightfully rural look

One way of including vegetables in a cottage garden is to grow them in a special patch of their own tucked in behind flowers and shrubs. At Peartwater Cottage, Somerset, the vegetables grow in the furthest corner of the garden. A grass path leads you through cottage-garden borders which blend gently into the vegetable plot.

which is especially suitable for a cottage garden surrounded by open countryside. This way of growing vegetables has been used at the garden of Peartwater Cottage in Somerset, and the result is a natural 'link' between the flower garden and the surrounding open countryside. At Water-meadows, also in Somerset, the garden is rather larger and allows for a good-sized patch of vegetables to be tucked into a triangular bed with roses and flowers at one end, screening the crops from the house. Here they have devised a most effective rustic birdscarer. Two pieces of mirror, fixed back-to-back, are suspended from a tripod of garden canes in the centre of the plot. As the mirrors rotate in the wind, flashes of light dart across the garden.

THE MIXED BORDER
Another method of including fruit and vegetables in a garden is to blend them into a mixed border with flowers and shrubs in the traditional

manner. This way has been chosen at Sticky Wicket in Dorset (see page 68), where the prettiest varieties of vegetables such as artichokes, red orache, the red-leaved beetroot 'Bull's Blood' (which produces perfectly good edible beet) are teamed with flowers of strongly contrasting shapes. Here, the vegetables act as colourful or architectural foliage plants to 'break up' the floral display. You could also include coloured versions of more popular vegetables, for example, red cabbage, frilly red lettuce such as 'Lollo Rosso' or 'Salad bowl' (which make neat edging plants for a

At this Devon cottage, garden crops have been chosen for their decorative qualities. Planted at the back of the border, they make a good background for flowers when viewed from the house. Here, tall silvery-leaved artichokes, and ferny asparagus foliage are joined by huge leaves of rhubarb. The pair of lovely old earthenware forcing pots were once used to cover the rhubarb plants in spring to produce tender early stems for the table.

path), purple Brussels sprouts, purple climbing beans, and rhubarb chard (a striking red and purple version of the better known Swiss chard); or train squashes, marrows or outdoor cucumbers up a tripod of rustic poles. Fruit trees and bushes are very easy to incorporate into flowerbeds as you can use them towards the back of a border as you would flowering trees or shrubs. Modern fruit trees on dwarfing rootstocks are very helpful here, as they will never get too big. Large fruit trees make good specimens for planting in a lawn, or you could grow espalier-trained fruit trees on cordons supported by stakes as a screen to divide off part of the garden. In either case you can use the tree as a support for climbers such as clematis.

THE ORNAMENTAL VEGETABLE GARDEN

The third way of incorporating edible crops into a garden is to create an ornamental vegetable garden that becomes a main feature – perhaps one of several 'gardens within a garden'. The original ornamental vegetable gardens – potagers – were not cottage garden creations at all, but the very

It is not difficult to create an ornamental fruit and vegetable garden in a small space, and still grow a useful quantity of interesting crops. To achieve the ornamental look, vegetables are planted in a geometric pattern based round central paths intended to facilitate cultivation and picking as well as contribute to the design. Adjacent crops are planned to contrast attractively in shape, colour or texture to make the most of the variety of plant forms available, and trained fruit trees and crops growing on arches contribute a change of height to the area. On the productivity side, the crops chosen are those which not only look nice but which also give the most edible produce from a small space or over a long picking season, such as runner beans and welsh onions, or taste best eaten fresh from the garden, like courgettes, 'Lollo Rosso' lettuce and Florence fennel. Coloured varieties of everyday vegetables, such as purple sprouts, also help to enliven a practical scheme.

grand vegetable gardens of French stately homes several centuries ago. However, small versions look very much at home in cottage gardens, and are becoming increasingly popular. The essence of a successful ornamental vegetable garden is that plants are not grown in rows but in a pattern of small blocks. The beds may be quite formal, with intricate patterns outlined in dwarf box or lavender like an Elizabethan knot garden, and each area filled with a different sort of vegetable. Or, more informally, the pattern can be marked out in sand, with gravel paths running between the beds, and the different crops allowed to spill over the edges and overlap with each other.

A superb example of an ornamental vegetable garden is that at Barnsley House in Gloucestershire. Here, the vegetable garden is divided into four squares, each of which is filled with an arrangement of square or oblong beds each planted with a different crop, and with old-brick paths running between them. The beds are kept small enough to permit hoeing and planting to be done from the path, without treading on the soil.

At Rosemary Verey's ornamental vegetable garden at Barnsley House, Gloucestershire, added interest has been created in the ornamental vegetable garden by placing Victorian-style arches over an old brick path. Instead of the more usual covering of trained fruit trees, here tall sunflowers have been planted between the arches to make a fascinating pattern which is best appreciated by walking through it.

The gardens' owner and designer, author Rosemary Verey, has two hints for making an ornamental vegetable garden that 'works'. One is to design the planting scheme to make the best use of different colours, textures and heights so that the crops form an attractive picture from any angle, and throughout most of the year. Leeks and Brussels sprouts, for instance, make a good combination, being similar in colour but very different in shape and texture. In another bed, trained apple trees are surrounded by a carpet of variegated strawberry foliage to add interest. But in a small space, a bed planted with any of the prettier vegetables such as carrots (for feathery foliage), rhubarb chard, red lettuce, and a tripod of canes growing climbing beans would make quite an attractive border on its

Neatly clipped box provides an interesting all-year-round edging in the ornamental vegetable garden at Barnsley House. Some beds are surrounded by low dwarf 'hedges', while others have a row of clipped bobbles. At the intersections of some of the main paths, focal points are provided by larger, shaped box trees. The box plants are clipped once a year, in late summer, to maintain their shape, and are well fed throughout the growing season.

The garden at Barnsley House is designed to look attractive and provide useful crops of fruit and vegetables over most of the year. The pattern of paths provides ready access to the beds which are small enough to be planted, weeded and harvested without having to tread on the soil. A lot of thought goes into planning which crops go into adjacent beds – height, colour, shape and texture are all taken into account. And as soon as a bed is emptied it is replanted immediately to avoid leaving empty gaps that would spoil the design.

own. The second essential is that the ground should never be left empty; as fast as one crop is cleared, the next lot of plants – lettuce, cabbage, etc. – should be ready to go in straight away.

A specially attractive feature of the vegetable garden at Barnsley is the arched walk, which currently is covered with marrows, with giant sunflowers thrusting up between the metal hoops. Such arches were used by the Victorians for growing trained fruit trees, vines or other climbing plants. Nowadays they are becoming popular again, and are a useful way of growing fruit trees ornamentally, even if you do not have room for a fruit and vegetable garden as such.

On a much smaller scale, a few ornamental vegetable beds have been

This bed at Knapp Lane Farmhouse, in Somerset, has a distinctly old-world cottage-economy air about it, with its 'bit of everything' planting of flowers, herbs, fruit and vegetables. By the time the plants have grown up a bit more the overall effect will be very soft and charming, with a blend of different leaf shapes, plant forms, and flower colours.

At Knapp Lane Farmhouse there are a number of different 'gardens within the garden', and one such ornamental area is devoted to edible crops. The central bed here has produced a crop of miniature Cos lettuce – the last row of which is still present – and will shortly be filled with a neat row of runner beans grown up traditional beanpoles. In the border to the right, a mixture of rhubarb, herbs and other vegetables are mingled with small shrubs and flowers.

incorporated into the garden at Knapp Lane Farmhouse, in Somerset – a cottage garden which includes several distinctive 'gardens within a garden'. These are much less formal than the ornamental vegetable garden at Barnsley House, and fit in very well with the ambience of the cottage and its garden.

Old Varieties of Vegetables

If you are growing vegetables primarily to eat, then modern varieties are almost certainly going to be your best bet – they are generally heavier cropping than old varieties, and many of them are suitable for freezing. However, if you want authenticity and the curiosity value of 'growing your own antiques', it is now possible to get seed of some of the old-fashioned varieties once again.

You could for instance try broad bean 'Aquadulce', introduced in 1844 and still a popular garden variety today. Or French bean 'Mont d'Or', which dates back to 1882 yet has the modern virtue of stringlessness. 'Painted Lady' runner bean has recently reappeared on many seed firms' lists; it has red and white flowers, which give it its name and make it a worthy candidate for the flower border. The beetroot 'Bull's Blood' is an old variety, though quite how old is not certain. It is worth growing both

Brassica plants and leeks make an attractive combination in an ornamental vegetable garden in Oxfordshire, as the plants are similar in colour but very different in shape and texture. Even if space is limited, alternate rows of the two crops will make an attractive feature, as well as supplying large quantities of useful vegetables for the table.

for its bright red leaves, which are good for flower arranging, and for the edible beetroots. Perpetual spinach was first introduced in 1869, and is still a very useful vegetable because it doesn't go to seed as readily as ordinary spinach. Plenty of the brassicas date back to the last century – 'Early Purple' sprouting broccoli, the red cabbage 'Red Drumhead', 'Wheeler's Imperial' and 'Harbinger' spring cabbages, the 'Ormskirk' savoys, and

Although the early cottage gardeners were restricted to growing large apple trees, we can select from a wide variety of different shapes and sizes thanks to modern dwarfing rootstocks. Here, apples have been trained to cover a framework of stakes, forming a natural divide across the ornamental vegetable garden at Barnsley House. To add to the interest, as well as making the most productive use of the space, marrows have been allowed to clamber up through the branches. Any varieties of trailing squashes, courgettes or outdoor cucumbers can be grown up a frame very successfully. It saves space compared to the traditional method of letting them run all over the ground, and prevents the fruits from rotting, which happens easily if they are resting on the soil.

'Purple Cape' and 'Late Queen' cauliflowers to name but a few. 'Purple Queen' is unusual in that it has bright purple curds, which taste nutty and buttery – far better than any white cauliflower. You can still get 'Telegraph' cucumbers to grow in your greenhouse (introduced in 1897), and 'Cottager's' kale (1885), which has beautiful mauve highlights to its foliage. Or for something very different, try the extraordinary kohl rabi 'Purple Vienna', which look like mauve tennis balls with leaves (first introduced in 1860). Older still is the Scotch flag, or 'Musselburgh' leek, dating from 1834. Some Victorian lettuce varieties are still very popular – the tiny 'Tom Thumb' dates from 1885, and the red-tinged 'Continuity' from 1900. The best-flavoured lettuce available today, 'Little Gem', was first introduced in 1905. Cantaloup melons were popular crops with Victorian gardeners, and several are still available today to grow under glass, such as 'Hero of Lockinge' and 'Blenheim Orange'. 'Snowball' turnip dates back to 1869, the giant pumpkin 'Mammoth' to 1860, 'Early Horn' carrot to 1834, and 'Ailsa Craig' onion to 1899, but one of the oldest varieties still available today must be the winter radish 'Long Black Spanish', which can be traced back to 1783.

Seed of some old-fashioned vegetable varieties is occasionally available by mail order from some seed firms. There is also a British organization (the National Centre for Organic Gardening – the old Henry Doubleday Research Association) who will 'lend' seed of old varieties to members on condition that they return the loan at the end of the season, by saving some seed from the plants they have grown to send back. There are also any number of enthusiasts keeping the old varieties alive. One cottage gardener 'collects' old beans, and grows a few every year in her vegetable plot to help keep the seed in circulation.

Old Varieties of Fruit

It is interesting to discover that many of the fruits we still grow today are in fact quite old varieties. 'Cox's Orange Pippin', for instance, which is still a favourite eating apple, was first discovered as a chance seedling growing in a cottage garden in 1855, while the best-known cooker, 'Bramley's Seedling' was similarly found in Nottinghamshire in 1809. Some of the most interesting old apple varieties still available include 'Ashmead's Kernel' (1685), a well-flavoured dessert apple that stores well; 'Court Pendu Plat', an eating apple with aromatic flesh, which is thought to date back to Roman times; 'Ribston Pippin' (1707), which has green and red striped fruit, and is said to be one of the best-tasting apples; 'James Grieve', the popular dual-purpose cooking and eating apple (introduced in 1893); and 'Worcester Pearmain' (1873). Of the plum family, the 'Green Gage' is amongst the oldest still in cultivation – it has been grown in Britain at least since 1724; the popular 'Victoria' plum first appeared in 1840 as a chance seedling in a Sussex garden; and 'Czar' was named in honour of the Czar of Russia, who made a visit to Britain in the year of its introduction, 1874.

The most important event in recent years is the development of dwarfing tree rootstocks. This means that you no longer need a lot of space to grow a fruit tree, or to wait ten years before it starts fruiting. Virtually all kinds of fruit trees are now available on dwarfing rootstock, enabling them to be grown in a cottage garden as a conventional small tree in a lawn or fruit garden, as an ornamental tree in a border, or as a fruiting hedge (by planting cordons or espaliers in a row and training them onto supports). Many old-fashioned varieties are also available from some of the nurseries specialising in fruit, and some will even propagate scarce old varieties for you on request. The place to find such firms is among the small advertisements at the back of gardening magazines.

4

Working with Colour

There is a commonly held view among gardeners that flowers cannot 'clash', because they are all natural colours. Not everyone, however, would agree with this. Some people particularly dislike certain colour combinations such as pink and yellow in a border, and others are not prepared to entertain bright colours like red or orange in the garden at all. So although the early cottagers would have created a largely random colour scheme by planting flowers wherever there was room, today we often prefer to plan the use of colour to some extent. One reason is that we have a very much wider choice of plant material available to us, in a vast range of colours. We also frequently have much bigger gardens to plan for.

Mauvey pinks and purple combine with brilliant yellow to create an exciting colour scheme in a large herbaceous border. There is just enough green between adjacent groups of flowers to separate them visually.

It is no coincidence that many of the cottage gardens in which colour is used particularly effectively are those belonging to artists. The principles involved in other fields of composition are very helpful in putting plants together to create a garden. But you don't have to be an artist to make colour work well for you. In the garden it is very easy to rectify mistakes by moving plants round until you hit a winning combination – a lot of people simply allow their garden to 'evolve' in this way over a good many years. But knowing a little of the theory and what has worked for other people can save time and effort. And once 'hooked' on colour, some people never stop experimenting with new plant associations and get a lot of enjoyment out of constantly altering the 'picture' they have 'composed' with their plants.

Using Colour – The Theory

People with an artistic background can instinctively pick colours that will team well together and create the desired effect, but for those who are not quite so sure, a few minutes spent looking at an artist's colour wheel can be very useful. This shows the relationships of different colours to each other, and helps you to pick different combinations of colours that 'go' together at a glance. You can have monochromatic schemes, i.e. different tones of the same colour; contrasting colours, such as purple and yellow or red and green, which are found opposite each other on the wheel; harmonizing colours, such as yellow and green or blue and purple, which are directly next to each other on the wheel; or triadic colours, such as blue, red and yellow, which are chosen from three equally spaced segments of the wheel. Choose less of the brighter colours and more of the paler ones if you want a restful result, and reverse the order if you want to create a 'riot of colour'.

But there are other factors to consider when choosing and using colours – backgrounds for instance. Colours are affected by the colour of their background; the same flower may be made to look very different depending on its situation or the other plants you put with it. You might choose to brighten a dark fence with a planting of white or light colours which will show up well against it. Conversely darker colours will show up best against a white painted wall. You can easily test the effect by holding a handful of flowers or illustrations cut from a catalogue up against each other, or by placing them in front of a cloth the same shade as the lawn, fence, wall or whatever else they will be seen against, before committing yourself to buy. Or, if it is practical, you can stand your chosen plants in situ for a few days and move them around before making up your mind which combinations to plant where.

Advancing and receding colours are useful to know about if you want to create an illusion of space in a small garden – they are used to great effect in many artists' cottage gardens, often without the owner even being conscious of having chosen them for that reason! Bright colours such as red,

A veritable riot of colour, this border includes all the colours a lot of gardeners would call 'clashing'. But here, red, pink, orange and yellow accentuate the colour of the brickwork behind the flowers, and recapture the spirit of the genuine old cottage garden.

Pink, mauve and silver create a warm and lively cottage-garden theme. The dark background of shrubs helps to make the bright colours and spiky shapes look even more dramatic.

orange and yellow (the colours that many gardeners either don't like or find difficult to place) appear to advance and bring the flowers closer to the onlooker. Receding colours – the dull blues and smoky mauves that appear on the horizon when you look over open countryside – make flowers seem further away. Green, interestingly, is considered to be halfway between these two opposites, which is useful as it forms the main background colour in any garden.

Using Colour in Practice

The traditional look of a cottage garden border planted in a wide range of randomly mixed colours is still popular. The difference is that, instead of just putting plants in anywhere there is room and leaving the colours to

Pink and orange are not colours that many people would put next to each other, but they form a perfect combination in this cottage-garden setting. *Astrantia* makes a good 'filler' flower in a border, helping to 'pull together' other shapes and colours.

chance, as the old cottagers did, people now tend to place plants rather more carefully so that even though there may be clashing colours in the same border, they are separated in some way.

One way to avoid a direct colour clash is to plant groups of plants whose colour either contrasts or harmonizes with those of their immediate neighbours. You could for instance put a purple-flowered plant between a pink and a yellow to split up colours that might otherwise clash. A more sophisticated technique is to graduate the colour from one plant to the next along the length of the bed.

Another way to tackle the problem of 'clashing' colours is to separate each group with green, red or silver foliage or with green or white flowers. Plants like *Alchemilla mollis*, *Nicotiana langsdorfii*, *Santolina*, red orache, *Artemisia*, and *Stachys* are very useful for this purpose. Or you can plan the border in such a way that spring-flowering plants such as comfrey, pulmonaria, and even bulbs alternate with summer-flowering kinds, so that their foliage makes a useful contribution to the scheme long after their flowers are over. You can also incorporate autumn-flowering plants such as nerines, *Amaryllis belladonna*, *Liriope muscari*, Japanese anemones, Michael-mas daisies, etc., in the same way.

However, if you like the effect of random planting, do not allow other people's opinions about clashing flowers to have any effect on your choice. There is no reason why you should not put whatever colours you like together if you are happy with the result. You have only to look at what comes up when you sow a mixed packet of seed of cottage favourites such as zinnias or antirrhinums to see that, provided the plants can relate to each other in some way, even the most 'outrageous' combination of colours can produce a perfectly happy result. There is nothing like a good mixture of bold colours to give a border a lively appearance and create a really traditional cottage-garden look.

Colour co-ordinated borders are currently popular as a way of ensuring successful colour combinations. You don't have to stick too rigidly to your chosen scheme, but by designing a border that is based loosely on a particular colour scheme you can get a blend of closely related colours that is very easy on the eye. It is also a good way of creating a sense of order in a large garden that could otherwise look cluttered and over-complicated. There are several different types of colour schemes you could opt for. You could have quite a broad spread of harmonizing colours such as yellow, green and orange, or pink, mauve and purple. You could go for contrasting colours such as purple and yellow, red and green, or blue and orange. Or you could restrict yourself to an even more limited range of colours by choosing a monochromatic border, using all the various shades of one colour. But as a general rule, the fewer colours you use, the more important it becomes to choose plants with interesting shapes and textures, both of foliage and flowers – and the more difficult it is to make the scheme 'work'. The most difficult of all are 'white' gardens – which actually look best if, as at Sissinghurst, a few very discreet hints of mauve are added as well as a huge selection of shades of green, grey, silver and cream to give depth to the scheme.

SEASONS OF COLOUR

In something as traditional as a cottage garden, a lot of people like to emphasize season colours – either all round the garden, or in special areas that take on particular importance at different times of year. In spring for instance, yellow is the traditional colour, easily provided by masses of daffodils, polyanthus and primroses, which are useful for planting on a bank or in a lawn. In summer, pinks, mauves and purples tend to be cottage garden favourites, since these are the common colours of many old

Yellow is traditionally the colour of spring, and forms the theme of this extravagant display of early summer bloom round a water garden in a cottage in West Sussex. But although the bed appears to be all yellow from a distance, a closer look reveals that other colours help to give depth to the display. Yellow primula, mimulus and *Lysimachia* are joined by touches of orange *Hemerocallis*, white arum lily and palest pink *Astilbe* and *Polygonum*. The dark background of foliage helps the bright colours stand out exceptionally well from the surrounding garden.

Pinks and mauves are popular in cottage
gardens as so many of the old roses and old-
fashioned flowers, such as *Dianthus*, foxgloves,
scabious and sweet Williams, come in those
colours.

Simple shapes and masses of randomly mixed
colour provide the traditional cottage-garden
look. And even in a limited space, it is possible
to grow a few annuals to provide colour all
summer long between a permanent planting of
shrubs or roses. By using annuals, it is very easy
to change a large part of your colour scheme
every year without touching the main structure
of the garden.

roses and other old-fashioned flowers traditionally planted with them. Brighter colours like orange, red and gold are more usually found in the autumn, provided by great drifts of dahlias and chrysanthemums, fruit such as apples, quinces and rosehips, berries of *Pyracantha* and *Cotoneaster*, and the autumn foliage of trees and shrubs such as *Rhus*, birch and *Fothergilla*. But whether you stick to the traditional seasonal colours or not, it is worth planning your colour schemes in the garden to give a bit of seasonal variation. For instance, a border of pink that is looking its best in spring may be all green foliage by midsummer, while in another part of the garden a bed of mauves and blues has taken over as the centre of attraction. Or you might have a border that looks interesting for a large part of the year, but where the spring colour scheme gradually changes to another in summer as a different set of plants comes into bloom.

VISUAL PARTNERSHIPS

One of the interesting things about colours is the way their character changes depending on the colours they are next to. You can test this indoors by looking at the effect of moving an ornament in front of different-coloured backgrounds. But it is perhaps even more noticeable when working with flowers in a garden, because plant shapes and textures vary as well. This allows you to use the same plant in different associations throughout the garden, or an area within it, to introduce a suggestion of

Mauve, purple, silver and white make a most attractive combination in this garden at Chilcombe House, Dorset, showing how much more important the different shapes and textures of both flowers and foliage become when you restrict yourself to a limited range of colours. Colours will take on completely different characters when mixed with different neighbours, allowing the same flowers to be used repeatedly throughout the garden in other plant associations without looking repetitious.

continuity – without it looking repetitious. At Chilcombe House, in Dorset, for instance, *Salvia* species are particular favourites, and their tall purple spikes take on an entirely different character when planted to grow up through roses, than when placed in a border based loosely on shades of purple, with white flowers for highlights and a leafy green background.

ADVANCING AND RECEDING COLOURS

Advancing and receding colours can be used to give the illusion of space in a small garden in the same way that artists use bright colours in the

One way of making a small garden appear larger is to 'borrow' a tip from artists and plan your garden so that the colours appear to recede gradually into the distance and create the illusion of depth. Place bright 'hot' colours such as red, yellow and orange close to the house as they 'draw' the eye to them; put softer colours like pink, light blue and lilac in the middle ground, and misty mauves, dark blues and purples towards the back.

foreground and misty mauves on the horizon to give depth to a two-dimensional landscape painting. This is something you see quite commonly in artists' cottage gardens, whether they have planned it or not. The trick is to place the brightest colours, such as red, orange and yellow, closest to the house (or to wherever you view that part of the garden from) and to fade the colours gradually through pinks and lilacs to purples as they get further away. It isn't essential to stick rigidly to the colour scheme – you could safely include pinks with your purples, so long as you choose the mauver shades rather than reddish pinks. In gardens where the distant view is of sky or water rather than rolling countryside, your furthest colours should trail off into glaucous grey instead of misty purple in order to achieve the effect of the garden receding into the distance.

Green is often the most undervalued colour in a garden, simply because there is so much of it. But by choosing flowers, seedheads and foliage with contrasting shapes, you can use green to create a most attractive 'cool' corner that can provide a visual break between busy areas of colour.

GREEN AS A COLOUR

Green is the one colour people tend to overlook in the garden, since it is so common. But it is worth thinking about it because, like any other colour, the way it is used will influence the final results. Large areas of lawn and dark green hedges are the traditional backgrounds for colourful beds of flowers. Blocks of green in the shape of trees and shrubs are particularly useful for giving the garden its shape. If these include a good collection of evergreens, then the garden will continue to look good throughout the winter as well – given a little extra interest in the form of winter-flowering plants and variegated foliage. Green flowers and foliage – especially if they have interesting shapes – make a superb foil for colourful or even clashing flowers, and are a good means of separating adjacent clumps of colour.

Plants with strikingly shaped leaves are particularly useful in situations where foliage is noticeable – for instance where they are seen against a background of stone, brickwork or gravel, as is common in many cottage gardens. They can also form a feature of their own, highlighted with a few white or lime green flowers and gold variegated ivies, to turn a dull or shady corner into a secret garden that makes a strong contrast to the bright colours of sunnier spots.

An Artist's Cottage Garden

A garden where there is a particularly interesting use of colours is that of Yew Tree Cottage in West Sussex. The owner designed the garden from scratch about twenty-five years ago, and although its not particularly large (about a third of an acre [0.13 hectares], of which just over half is at the rear of the cottage), it provides a constantly changing tableau of colour and interest virtually all year round.

The foundation of the garden is its evergreens, which form roughly a third of the total planting. Although these are not traditional cottage-garden plants, they help cut down the work and provide a permanent and unobtrusive framework. The back garden is divided into two parts: the main garden, which is visible from the house, and beyond it a separate piece of land reached via a short stone-flagged path running through natural woodland. This extra land was acquired later and 'tacked on' after the rest of the garden had been designed and planted. Once used as the vegetable plot, it is now a testing ground for all sorts of bright colours and

OPPOSITE
The view from the garden door out over the back garden of Yew Tree Cottage, West Sussex. Immediately outside is a small informal paved area, surfaced with a mixture of old bricks, pebbles and stone slabs, and incorporating an old wellhead, now covered over and turned into a seat. The picture is completed by a large, gnarled old quince tree whose umbrella-like shape frames the view of the garden and surrounding countryside. The bed in the foreground is planted with a mixture of ivies and rue to give evergreen interest all year round, while pink flowers provide later-spring colour. As the season progresses, the centre of interest moves further down the garden, where beds of summer flowers in pinks, mauves and purples merge gently into the farmland beyond. The boundary to one side of the garden is formed by an informal line of trees and shrubs, with a low buckthorn hedge across the end.

Past the end of the garden at Yew Tree Cottage lies a small piece of land, once used as a vegetable plot and now a 'semi-detached' herbaceous border. Reached via a short woodland walk, which keeps it entirely separate from the main garden, this is where the owner tries out brighter colour schemes and plant associations suitable for occasional rather than everyday viewing. The design is very simple. A straight path runs through a rose arch, between two equal-sized rectangular beds, to a seat on a raised stone plinth buried in foliage at the far end. Like the rest of the garden, this area is packed with ground-covering plants to keep maintenance work down.

RIGHT
From a raised seat at the top end of the detached flower garden in the woods, you can just see Yew Tree Cottage across the field next door – although the part of the garden seen here is not visible from the house. For this reason the owner feels able to try out more experimental colour schemes here than in the main garden. Touches of hot orange, yellow, and red are added to the mauves and purples for a more riotous display.

The main garden at Yew Tree Cottage has a colour scheme loosely based on pinks, mauves and purples. Bright, 'hot' colours are not used here, as they are felt by the owner to be too distracting. Evergreens, conifers and shrubs form the backbone of the garden, which has been designed with ease of maintenance in mind. Around them the ground is kept well filled with low spreading plants to smother out weeds.

Wide borders in front of a background framework of conifers, evergreen and deciduous shrubs characterize the planting at Yew Tree Cottage. Borders at least 6–7 ft (2 m) wide are essential if you are to be able to grow enough different plants to give continuity of colour over a long season without the bed looking 'bitty'. Here the colours are graduated so that brighter colours are placed nearer to the house, gradually fading in intensity as they get further away, helping to create an illusion of size in quite a small back garden.

plant combinations that the owner would not like to 'risk' in the main garden, which is permanently on view.

The main garden is laid chiefly to lawn with a shaped border round the edge. From the house this makes a pleasant scene that leads the eye out over the surrounding countryside. Immediately outside the garden door is a huge old fruiting quince tree whose umbrella shape frames the view of the garden, while beneath it an old wellhead and colourful flowerbed provide foreground interest. In the spring this bed is full of pink flowers, but as summer progresses it becomes more neutral in tone, and colour is then provided by pink, mauve and purple flowers in large beds towards the bottom of the garden.

The owner, as you might expect, is an artist, who has planned the colour scheme to make the smallish rear garden appear larger, and blend gently into the countryside beyond. Brightly coloured flowers such as yellow and orange are avoided as they would draw attention to themselves and away from the general view. Even the lawn contributes to the colour scheme; clovers and self-heal are allowed to flourish as their pink and mauve flowers look pretty in the summer, while broad-leaved weeds like plantain and daisies are removed. In all the borders, ground-covering plants such as hardy geraniums fill the space beneath shrubs and taller flowers, and are encouraged to 'smother' the soil, so that weeding can be kept to a minimum. The owner is a firm believer in planting large spreads of ground cover, which looks more effective in this situation than the traditional mixed cottage-garden planting. Despite this, the width of the borders – at least 6–7 ft (2 m) deep – enables a sufficient number of different plants to be grown to keep the colour going throughout the summer. Later flowering kinds are planted near the front of the borders so that they screen the foliage of early-flowering plants that have gone over.

Stonework and garden ornaments are a
particular passion of the owner of Yew Tree
Cottage, who has created several delightful
associations of plants and small architectural
features throughout the garden. Here, a few
stone slabs set into the soil, an old stone sink
backed by a small raised bed walled with
granite setts, a stoneware jar and some water-
worn pebbles make an attractive feature.

Just outside the kitchen door of Yew Tree
Cottage, is a paved area that houses a collection
of potted plants. The colour scheme follows that
of the rest of the garden – pink, mauve and
purple. And in keeping with the surroundings of
a 14th-century cottage, most of the containers
used here are old terracotta pots.

5

The Apothecary's Garden

If you look back far enough in history, you'll find that a large proportion of the original cottage garden plants were herbs. Not perhaps herbs as we think of them today, for culinary use, but in the wider sense of plants with a useful function to perform. In the days before supermarkets and chemists, or indeed prepared products of any kind, plants were used as medicines, toiletries, fabric dyes, insect repellants and air fresheners, not to mention love potions, deterrents against witchcraft and other even more spurious functions – as well as for flavouring food and drinks. Nowadays, even though we may not want to use the old herbs in the same ways as our forbears did, they are still very worthy additions to a cottage garden.

A formal herb garden in Buckinghamshire; here low hedges of herbs line the edges of the paths and the plants are laid out in straight rows. *Santolina* has been used in place of the more usual dwarf box as an edging plant. This must be kept regularly clipped as it grows much faster than box.

A scented corner is a lovely place to put a garden seat. In this garden, you can enjoy a combination of perfumes from roses, bronze fennel and lavender. It is a good idea to place low growing herbs such as marjoram, mint, and thyme just in front of the seat where you'll walk, as the scent of foliage plants is only released when the leaves are bruised or crushed.

Herbs in the Cottage Garden

Herbs can be incorporated into a cottage garden in a great many ways – they are incredibly versatile. Some gardeners have discovered the interest value to be gained from including a few useful plants such as woad, camphor or fleabane in among other flowers in a cottage garden. Such herbs are generally quite attractive plants, often with rather out-of-the-ordinary looks, so that they stand out even if they are not classically beautiful. Herb enthusiasts will often gather together a collection in a specially designed herb garden, while other gardeners grow their herbs in rows in the vegetable garden and treat them as a crop to be harvested like any other. (This is a good idea if you need a lot of something as you can cut large quantities without spoiling the look of your ornamental garden).

Any one of these methods, or a combination of all three, may be considered an authentic cottage-gardening technique. The only limiting factors for herbs are soil and situation – most herbs tend to prefer a well-drained soil and a sunny situation. However, growing them in poor soil or in a dryish site is said to produce a more concentrated aroma or flavour.

A SPECIALIST HERB GARDEN

One such specialist herb garden is to be found at Mill House in West Sussex. The herb garden, which is in a corner of the main garden, separated from it by old stone walls that once enclosed what was probably a pen for livestock, is semi-formal in style, paved with old bricks laid herringbone fashion, with spaces left between them at regular intervals for groups of plants. The collection is of medicinal and useful plants rather than culinary herbs, and includes some relatively little-grown herbs. Here are liquorice, which was once used for treating stomach ulcers; *Saponaria* (soapwort) for washing delicate fabrics; vervain (*Verbena officinalis*), once used for warding off witches; pennyroyal (*Mentha pulegium*) to repel fleas, and tansy (*Tanacetum major*) to repel flies; mandrake (*Mandragora officinarum*), the root of which was used for pain relief in the time of Alexander the Great – lengths of it were issued to his soldiers as part of their battle kit; wolf's bane (*Aconitum vulparia*), once used to poison wolves; sage for treating eye troubles and sore throats, self-heal (*Prunella vulgaris*), used by carpenters to stop cuts from bleeding; *Anthemis tinctoria* for dyeing fabric; *Atriplex hortensis* (mountain spinach or orache), used as a tonic at the end of

The herb garden at Mill House, West Sussex, is a specialist collection of medicinal and other useful herbs. The herb collection is separated from the rest of the garden by the old stone walls of what must once have been a pen for livestock. When the area was turned into a herb garden, a solid floor of brick was laid with evenly spaced gaps left for the different herbs to grow in small groups.

RIGHT
A collection of culinary herbs can be easily arranged to give aesthetic appeal by laying them out in a formal or semi-formal herb garden as seen here. Not only does it look pretty, making a good cottage-style alternative to a patio outside french windows or a kitchen door perhaps, but it is also a very practical idea as it enables you to gather herbs easily without getting your feet wet, whatever the weather. A hedge of low shrubs such as lavender provides a natural-looking boundary to the herb garden, though dry stone or brick walls could be used instead. Inside the garden, the planting scheme is designed so that neighbouring plants contrast as much as possible in shape, colour and texture of foliage, to make up for the small and often insignificant flowers of herbs.

The first place to think of planting climbers with scented flowers is round the door, where you'll get the most benefit from their perfume. At this Dorset cottage, they've chosen to use honeysuckle. Several different varieties are available, flowering at different times. If you want continuity of flowers – and scent – try planting both the early Dutch honeysuckle (*Lonicera periclymenum* 'Belgica') and the large red honeysuckle (*L. p.* 'Serotina') in the same spot. Between them, they will produce a succession of flowers from May to October.

the winter and which does apparently have a high vitamin C content; and orris (*Iris* 'Florentina'), whose roots, when harvested, dried and ground up, are scented and were used for perfuming linen. They are still commonly used to 'fix' the scent of potpourri.

The herb garden at Mill House has been designed to look as ornamental as possible. A stone birdbath and sundial provide focal points in the centre, and the pattern of bricks and the old stone walls make a good 'foil' for the plants. Though the basic colour is green, the herbs are planted to create maximum interest, with tall architectural plants like *Verbascum* and camphor distributed evenly round the garden, and the lower-growing, clump-forming kinds and those with more colourful flowers used as 'fillers' in between.

Scented Plants in the Cottage Garden

Scented gardens – collections of aromatic climbers, shrubs and flowers – are specially useful for people whose eyesight is poor, but in a cottage garden, aromatic plants are more commonly distributed throughout the garden so that you move from one scent to another as you walk round. This

BELOW
At a cottage in Somerset, scented-leaved pelargoniums on the windowsill create a lingering fragrance indoors, and act as a link with the herb collection and cottage garden outside. In common with most scented-leaved plants, scented pelargoniums must be touched before their perfume is released. The leaves of scented geraniums can be used to line a cake tin when baking a sponge so that the delicate aroma permeates the cake – and the kitchen at the same time.

gives you a better chance to enjoy each scent individually, without being overwhelmed by an over-rich mixture in any one place. Here are a few other general points on the placing of aromatic plants that are worth taking into account when planning a garden.

There is a difference in placing plants with scented flowers from those with scented leaves. The latter only release their fragrance when the leaves are crushed or slightly bruised, so they are best placed along the edges of paths or where you will brush past them or feel tempted to give them a squeeze as you go by. A warm sunny spot in a sheltered situation is required if you want to enjoy their perfume; the volatile oils vaporize better given warmth, and linger longer in still air. Scented flowers can be placed wherever you will get close enough to smell them. In placing scented flowers, be aware of the strength or lack of it in different kinds of flower; a little lavender goes a long way, whereas you need a good-sized patch of cowslips – unless they are very close to the edge of the path – to detect their scent at all! Remember that scented-leaved plants provide scent all the time they are in leaf, while those with scented flowers are obviously only scented while the flowers are open. It therefore pays to choose a selection of scented flowering plants to give continuity, as far as possible, through the changing seasons – plants like the winter-flowering shrubby honeysuckles (*Lonicera × purpusii* and *L. fragrantissima*), are specially useful in this respect.

Although scented plants should be used all round a cottage garden, there are a few special places where they are particularly valuable. One is by the front door. Jasmine, climbing roses and honeysuckle are the traditional favourites here, their scent can be enjoyed every time the door is opened, and some of the perfume is certain to find its way indoors. Archways are another popular place to put scented climbers such as honeysuckles and roses. It is perfectly practical to have an arch covered in scented flowers throughout most of the season by growing a rose and a honeysuckle together, or two or three different kinds of honeysuckle chosen to give a succession of flowers. (Choose the early and late Dutch honeysuckles, *Lonicera periclymenum* 'Belgica', which flowers in early summer and again in late summer, and 'Serotina', which flowers from midsummer to autumn, or the native woodbine, plain *Lonicera periclymenum*, which flowers from midsummer to early autumn.)

Paths are a good place for aromatic plants. Creeping plants such a thymes grow very happily in cracks between paving stones or bricks, as well as in gravel, and not only tolerate a certain amount of regular wear but also release their delightful fragrance whenever they are crushed. Chamomile is just as good for this, and both thymes and chamomile can be planted as aromatic 'lawns' in light well-drained soil. They won't take the regular heavy wear of a grass lawn, but can look charming located somewhere that only gets occasional use, and the scent when you walk on them is quite an experience. In a very special spot you might have a scented seat, like the one at Sissinghurst – a stone bench with a carpet of *Mentha requienii*, a low creeping species, growing in its hollow 'seat'.

Cottage windowsills are a good place for scented pot plants. In days gone by, cottagers used them to help combat the smells of cooking and damp, and to repel flies. The sort of plants grown on windowsills in those days would have been restricted to ones that did not mind low temperatures in winter, as of course there was no central heating. Scented-leaved pelargoniums may have survived, and certainly thrive in modern cottages. They come in many varieties with rose, spice, lemon, orange and even peppermint scents. Mint makes another good windowsill plant though most common sorts grow too tall and straggly after a short time unless they are regularly cut back (which they don't seem to mind). Eau de Cologne mint is a very nice plant, with darkish leaves and the characteristic eau de Cologne scent, but the authentic cottage-garden-windowsill mint is *Mentha × gentilis*, ginger mint, which has pretty golden-splashed leaves. A popular flowering plant which is hardly seen nowadays was mignonette (*Reseda odorata*). This is an annual that is thrown away after flowering. Ordinary zonal pelargoniums, which also have pleasantly scented leaves if touched, are probably one of the favourite cottage-windowsill plants.

HERBS AND AROMATIC PLANTS IN A FLOWER GARDEN
At Sticky Wicket in Dorset, a huge range of herbs and other aromatics of all sorts are grown, together with purely ornamental plants, in a most unusual kind of cottage garden. Here, instead of following the traditional cottage-

Pinks, thyme, violas and lavender make a good cottage combination in the round garden at Sticky Wicket, Dorset. The plants chosen create a pleasantly harmonious colour scheme, and add fragrance, bees and butterflies to the cottage-garden atmosphere.

A selection of herbs helps to set off purely ornamental plants and flowers at Sticky Wicket. The foliage of purple sage is used to break up large areas of flowers and makes a particularly pleasing background for pink hardy cranesbill. In the foreground is one of the catmints (*Nepeta*), which will attract both butterflies and cats given half a chance. Feverfew's daisy-like flowers are nicely offset by their own lime green foliage. The *Nigella* behind it was used in the past as an insect repellant. Behind that is variegated buddleia, which when it comes into flower will prove a great attraction for butterflies.

The round garden at Sticky Wicket is a cottage garden in terms of its planting style and the sorts of plants used – a mixture of shrubs, flowers and herbs – though the design is distinctly un-conventional. Gravel paths divide this circular garden into concentric rings and bisect it at right angles. Marking the very centre is a sundial set in an aromatic chamomile lawn, which has proved to be surprisingly hard-wearing.

garden formula, the owners – who are garden designers by profession – have made a round garden. It is designed rather like a dartboard, with circular paths dividing it into a series of concentric rings bisected by straight paths that run through the centre of the circle. In between the paths are arc-shaped beds. The owners use these different beds as 'testing grounds' for new plant associations, but nevertheless prefer to keep the cottage-style planting and plants, so despite the unusual layout the general effect is still that of a cottage garden. Round the outside of the garden, taller shrubs create an aura of privacy; most of the kinds chosen here are native species and their close garden relatives as the intention is to blend the garden into the surrounding, very rural, countryside. Further into the garden, a mixture of roses, shrubs, climbers, herbs and old-fashioned flowers are mixed together, including a good proportion of scented plants throughout. Aromatic plants such as lavender, thyme, pinks, purple sage (*Salvia officinalis* 'Purpurascens'), different species of *Santolina*, *Nicotiana*, feverfew, and catmints are specially conspicuous in midsummer, together with a few unusual plants such as the old 'Painted Lady' sweet pea,

In a bed that follows roughly one colour scheme, such as the pink and red scheme shown here at Sticky Wicket, it is particularly important to make a good contrast in shape. The giant alliums and artichoke heads are the main architectural shapes here, with a clump of gone-to-seed leeks making nice peaks in the background. Bronze fennel provides a misty purple haze on the right-hand side of the picture and in the background tall spikes of pink-flowering *Spiraea salicifolia* helps the cultivated garden to blend into the surrounding countryside.

growing on sticks, and the chamomile lawn that surrounds the sundial at the very centre of the garden. A general view across the round garden gives the impression that it is full of flowers, but in fact the flowering plants are interspersed with foliage – silver, grey, and red – so that each group of flowers is seen against a good background. Wherever possible, flowering plants with interesting foliage have been chosen, so that they contribute something to the scheme even when they are not in flower. And although at first glance it looks as though the whole garden is planned on a colour scheme of mauves and pinks, each arc-shaped bed actually has a colour scheme of its own, which is designed to give the impression of a gradually changing blend of colours as you walk round the garden – very clever, and extremely effective!

Which Plants to Choose

It is surprising to discover just how many of the plants we now think of as purely ornamental were grown for practical purposes in the old cottage gardens. Many had more than one use. Sempervivums, for instance, were commonly grown in many parts of the country on the roofs of old cottages to protect them from lightning. The same plants pounded up with lard, were an old country remedy for chilblains, while the juice was used neat to cure warts. It is also rather sad to find how many more of the old useful plants – such as camphor, once used to protect clothes from moths – have largely disappeared from our gardens because their original functions have long since been replaced by modern products. The following is a selection of the many interesting and unusual plants with outmoded uses that are well worth including in a modern cottage garden.

PLANTS TO REPEL INSECTS Their leaves or shoots were usually dried and tucked into drawers or hung up in cupboards. Camphor (*Balsamita major tomentosum*) against moths; pennyroyal (*Mentha pulegium*) for fleas and ants; mugwort (*Artemisia vulgaris*) and wormwood (*Artemisia absinthium*) as general insecticides; fleabane (*Pulicaria dysenterica*), the leaves were burnt to drive away fleas; tansy (*Tanacetum major*), the fresh crushed leaves were used to deter flies; cotton lavender (*Santolina chamaecyparissus*), fresh sprigs were used to brush clothes to repel insects; mint, a few sprigs in a jam jar on a kitchen windowsill is still a good remedy for keeping flies away.

DYE PLANTS The latin name 'tinctoria' indicates that a plant was once used for dyeing. Alkanet (*Anchusa officinalis*), the root yields a red dye; bloodroot (*Sanguinaria canadensis*), dandelion, dyer's chamomile (*Anthemis tinctoria*), dyer's woodruff (*Asperula tinctoria*), dyer's broom (*Genista tinctoria*), golden rod, marigold, and dyer's safflower (*Carthamus tinctorius*), all produce red and yellow dyes; dyer's weld (*Reseda luteola*) gives a yellow dye; woad leaves were fermented to produce the blue dye favoured by Ancient Britons.

MEDICINAL PLANTS Arnica for external use on bruises and sprains; feverfew for migraine; heartsease flowers were made into cough syrup; horseradish was rubbed on insect bites and stings; houseleek (*Sempervivum*) juice was used for burns, warts, and mixed with lard for chilblains; lady's mantle (*Alchemilla mollis*) for treating female disorders, and the juice was used to treat acne; lavender as smelling salts for fainting fits; lungwort (*Pulmonaria*) to treat lung disorders, because the spotted pattern of the leaves was thought to resemble a lung; an infusion of sage was used as mouthwash and gargle for sore throats; clary (*Salvia sclarea*) seeds were made into eyewash; dill to treat flatulence; elder flower tea for colds; lime flower tea to induce sleep; chamomile (*Chamaemelum nobile*) tea was taken to prevent nightmares; elecampane (*Inula helenium*) for chest complaints; valerian (*Valeriana officinalis*) as a tranquillizer.

AIR FRESHENERS These were particularly necessary in old cottages with poor sanitation and no damp-proof courses. Dried flowers of lavender were tied up in linen sachets and put in drawers to perfume linen, and were also placed in bowls to freshen rooms; orris (*Iris* 'Florentina') roots smell of violets when dried and ground – this powder was used to perfume linen or added to potpourri to mask the musty smell of damp; roseroot (*Rhodiola rosea*) was used in the same way – its dried and ground roots smell of roses; woodruff (*Galium odoratum*) stems and leaves when dried smell of new-mown hay.

By interspersing flowering plants with good foliage ones, you can achieve the appearance of a garden full of flowers even though fewer are actually in bloom than you think. Here, golden marjoram and rue in the foreground break up large drifts of violas and lavender. Further back domes of silvery *Santolina* and daisy-like feverfew make a nice contrast in shape to the loose, bushier shapes of purple sage and the surrounding flowering plants.

COSMETICS OR TOILETRIES Anise (*Pimpinella anisum*) seeds were chewed to sweeten the breath; an infusion of chamomile (*Chamaemelum nobile*) was used as a rinse to brighten blond hair; rosemary, similarly used as a rinse for dark hair; elder was used to make skin preparations; field scabious (*Knautia arvensis*) for removing freckles; soapwort (*Saponaria officinalis*) as a shampoo; wild strawberry fruit were rubbed on skin to whiten it and on teeth to remove discoloration; an infusion of yarrow was used to clear oily skin; eau de Cologne mint to make perfumed toilet water.

FLAVOURINGS FOR ALE OR WINE Plants were commonly grown in pub gardens for this purpose. Avens (*Geum urbanum*) and alecost (*Balsamita major tanecetoides*) as a flavouring for ale; woodruff for wine cups; clove pink (*Dianthus caryophyllus*) for mulled wine.

OTHER PURPOSES Goat's rue (*Galega officinalis*) was sometimes used to clot milk for cheesemaking; soapwort (*Saponaria*) for washing delicate fabrics; teazel heads were used to 'tease' wool to raise a nap; horsetail (*Equisetum arvense*) for polishing pewter.

In a modern cottage garden it is also well worthwhile including herbs and aromatic plants which offer other useful benefits, such as attracting bees or scenting the garden, or those of culinary value.

SCENTED FLOWERS Climbing plants – honeysuckle, woodbine (*Lonicera periclymenum*), early Dutch honeysuckle (*L.p.* 'Belgica'), and late Dutch honeysuckle (*L.p.* 'Serotina'); *Clematis flammula* and *C. rehderiana*, the latter has the scent of cowslips; jasmine (*Jasminum officinale*); climbing roses. Shrubs – shrubby honeysuckles (*Lonicera × purpusii* and *L. fragrantissima*); roses, especially old-fashioned kinds; daphne; witch hazel (*Hamamelis mollis*); *Mahonia japonica*, which has the scent of lily-of-the-valley; *Viburnum farreri*, *V. × burkwoodii*, *V. carlesii* and *V. × juddii*; mock orange (*Philadelphus*); laburnum; lilac. Flowers – note that many modern varieties of annuals do not have any scent even though their old-fashioned counterparts may be noted for it, such as sweet peas and tobacco plant – lavender; tobacco plant (*Nicotiana affinis*); sweet peas – old-fashioned varieties such as 'Painted Lady', old-fashioned seed mixtures and a few modern named varieties can be relied on for scent; mignonette (*Reseda odorata*); pinks – old-fashioned varieties are clove-scented; Brompton stock; night-scented stock; wallflower; evening primrose (*Oenothera biennis*); lily-of-the-valley (*Convallaria majalis*).

SCENTED LEAVES Curry plant (*Helichrysum italicum*) is fairly strongly curry-scented; scented-leaved pelargoniums in a big choice of varieties each with a different scent – orange, lemon, rose, cloves, cinnamon, peppermint, etc.; myrtle (*Myrtus communis*); sweet briar (*Rosa eglanteria*) leaves are apple-

Although they would not have been used in real old cottage gardens, Hybrid Tea roses are sometimes included in modern planting schemes, especially if they are scented cultivars. They are normally included with other cottage garden plants in a mixed border rather than being planted in beds on their own. Here, feverfew and variegated apple mint have been used.

Roses and catmint (*Nepeta*) make a striking combination of both colour and scent. It is common to underplant old roses with low herbaceous plants in cottage gardens so that you have something in flower when the roses stop blooming in midsummer. If you happen to have unscented varieties of Hybrid Tea roses in your garden, you can use the same idea to add scent, by underplanting them with fragrant plants like catmint or lavender.

scented, especially after rain; zonal geranium (*Pelargonium × hortorum*) leaves have a distinctive geranium smell.

PLANTS FOR POTPOURRI Ground orris root; ground roseroot (*Rhodiola rosea*); lavender flowers and leaves; scented-leaved geranium; rose petals; angelica leaves; bergamot leaves; pot marigold petals; violets.

PLANTS TO ATTRACT BEES Anise hyssop (*Agastache foeniculum*); catmint and catnip (*Nepeta* species), which also tend to attract cats; lavender; borage; viper's bugloss (*Echium vulgare*); lemon balm (*Melissa officinalis*).

PLANTS TO ATTRACT BUTTERFLIES Marjoram; buddleia; *Sedum spectabile*; dame's violet (*Hesperis matronalis*); red valerian (*Centranthus ruber*).

EDIBLE FLOWERS Borage flowers for use in summer drinks such as Pimm's, or frozen whole in ice cubes; nasturtium flowers can be stuffed with cream cheese or used in salads; pot marigold (*Calendula officinalis*) petals can be used in salads and to colour rice instead of saffron; rose petals can be made into jelly or wine.

PLANTS FOR CANDYING Borage flowers; violet flowers; angelica stems.

EDIBLE SEEDS For sprinkling on bread before baking – opium poppy (*Papaver somniferum*) and cornfield poppy (*P. rhoeas*); or cakes – aniseed (*Pimpinella anisum*) or caraway (*Carum carvi*).

6
Recreating the Old-Fashioned Garden

The earlier chapters of this book are full of ideas for planting combinations and architectural features that help to make up a traditional, old-fashioned cottage garden. But just adding old-fashioned plants or garden features will not guarantee a garden that looks genuinely old-fashioned. It also takes a bit of special magic to project the feeling of antiquity into a modern garden, and perhaps a rekindling of the same spirit with which the early cottagers created their gardens. Here are some of the special tips that have been successfully used by many cottage gardeners who have managed to give their gardens that elusive old-fashioned ambience.

Ancient climbing roses on the wall, a slightly shaggy daisy studded lawn, and a delightful jumble of different plants growing randomly together all help create an old-world atmosphere at this cottage in Suffolk.

This cottage in West Sussex, is listed in the Domesday Book; the garden is rather more recent, however, having been planned and planted within the last few years. In the huge border in front of the house grow all the traditional cottage-garden favourites, such as roses, delphiniums, and peonies, which provide a good mixture of colours throughout the summer.

FEATURES AND MATERIALS

The early cottagers were very good at making do without expensive plants and materials; they used what they could find for free. Many successful cottage gardeners today have done the same thing, but as a way of adding 'atmospheric' features to the garden. They have re-used old bricks, stone paving slabs, sinks and chimneypots for garden paths, paving and plant containers. Or hoarded stones or entire porches when old buildings in their village were demolished. They have closed off old wellheads for safety and used them as interesting architectural features. And searched hedgerows, farm sales, rubbish dumps and village jumbles for 'finds' which, with a little effort and imagination, have been turned into ornaments that add considerable old-world character to their gardens. Even garden rubbish has been converted into something 'atmospheric' – fallen tree trunks used as an edging for a footpath through a wild garden, or willow prunings made into an arbour. Alternatively, there are builders' merchants that specialize in reclaiming old materials. Or you can do your hunting in

Old-fashioned plants growing close together, aged plant containers and a background of ancient brick walls are the perfect combination to suggest an old-world ambience. And a natural design with touches of formality completes the illusion – even if the garden is not all that old at all. This one, in Buckinghamshire, was planted up about four years ago.

antique and junk shops, or rural craft centres. But however you come by your 'find', it still takes flair to position it well and to combine it with the right plants.

CONCEALING THE MODERN WORLD

Modern life has a way of intruding into even the remotest rural community. But successful cottage gardeners try to preserve the fantasy of their old-world surroundings by masking modern intrusions. TV aerials, for instance, may be banished to the attic, and washing lines hidden or taken down after use. Modern garden furniture can be avoided in favour of simple wooden benches, which can be left outside all year round, and made more comfortable by scattering cushions on them when they are in use. Sheds, oil tanks and dustbins can be screened off by trelliswork smothered with climbers, or a strategically placed border of evergreen shrubs. And if the garden has a view over a modern housing estate, pylons or telegraph poles, then a group of trees and shrubs can usually be planted to conceal

Climbers help this weatherboarded cottage in Bedfordshire to blend with its surroundings, and although a good mixture of colours are present they manage not to clash. Climbing roses and *Clematis montana rubens* are combined with other traditional cottage-garden plants, including an elder bush, variegated box, aquilegia and snow-in-summer, interspersed with self-sown hardy annual poppies to create a natural-looking, well-filled carpet of colour.

Grassy paths are all that remain of a lawn at this old cottage in Norfolk; plants take up all the rest of the space. Here, a surrounding of native trees provides a suitable backdrop to the ornamental cultivars of shrubs and flowers within the garden. The tallest trees and shrubs are planted round the perimeter of the garden, providing a sheltered area in their midst for smaller, more delicate flowers which are more easily seen from the house against a framework of foliage.

them. Conversely, while such modern monstrosities can be hidden, it is also possible to accentuate a rural view, perhaps by cutting a dip in a hedge or removing a tree, or by making a 'frame' of trees and shrubs to draw attention to it, thus creating the illusion that your garden is surrounded by rolling countryside, even if it isn't.

Old-Fashioned Planting

You can recreate a traditional planting scheme, even without restricting yourself to historic cottage-garden plants, by following the same sort of formula the early cottage gardeners used. Cottage gardens incorporate a blend of formal and informal plantings. In the old gardens, there would be straight rows of plants lining the edges of a path, or 'special' flowers planted in a row in front of a wall. In certain situations, formal beds with straight

This Somerset garden contains a real old-fashioned cottage-garden selection, chosen simply because they are the owner's favourite plants. The very old and beautifully gnarled apple trees near the house have been left for their shape and antiquity; they no longer give very much fruit. There is a profusion of old roses – and a few Hybrid Teas, self-sown foxgloves, pinks, sweet Williams, *Aquilegia*, *Geum*, *Achillea* and *Geranium*, creating a pleasant patchwork effect. There is no lawn in this part of the garden, just narrow winding paths from which to view and enjoy the plants.

edges would be used – in a front garden, or a formal herb garden, a walled garden or traditional vegetable plot perhaps. Elsewhere a very much more natural scheme would prevail with trees, shrubs and flowers allowed to seed themselves or simply to spread into huge clumps over the years.

In a modern garden you can still blend formal and informal designs together very successfully. Formal knot gardens, herb gardens, arched fruit trellises and paved areas with containers, for instance, contrast well with informal wild gardens and wildflower lawns, natural-looking water features, woodland walks and old-fashioned roses underplanted with ground-covering flowers. In informal areas, it is important to make plants look as randomly planted as possible. But many cottage gardeners in fact plan their 'random' planting with great care to ensure adjacent plants offer a pleasing contrast in colour, texture and shape, rather than the mess that could easily result. Whatever you choose to plant, though, the essence is to keep all the soil covered. Carpets of creeping plants – including bulbs in spring – overhung by larger shrubs, and a background of taller trees if the garden is big enough, provide a tiered effect which keeps the garden looking permanently well filled.

NATURAL EFFECTS

Whereas many gardeners strive to achieve perfect results with well-manicured lawns, carefully staked flowers and correctly spaced trees and

A garden that looks authentically old fashioned appears to have 'happened' naturally, but in fact it takes quite careful planning to achieve a casual yet pretty effect. Many modern cottage-owners have evolved their own 'rules' over a lifetime of gardening. Some, for instance, like to plant native species of trees and shrubs round the edge of the garden, keeping the smaller flowers and old-fashioned roses to beds within the sheltered area in the centre. Climbers on the cottage wall, especially round the door, are a very traditional feature. Lawns on the other hand are not – instead, old gardens had a carpet of flowers and plants planted in informal groups of randomly mixed colours at the front of the cottage. Today's gardener often prefers to separate 'clashing' colours with cool whites or greens, for a more harmonious look.

shrubs, a true cottage garden relies on imperfections to create its character. Plants are encouraged to grow naturally, with tall flowers often left unstaked to blend romantically together in a border, or to flow forwards over the edge of the lawn. Trees and shrubs planted too close together may be left to form a natural group. Fruit trees may be left unpruned; old apple trees, whose lower boughs have been dragged down by the weight of successive crops, can be supported by Y-shaped wooden props. Lawns can be allowed to sprout daisies and other 'weeds' few modern-style gardeners would tolerate; and they can also be left to grow longer. Paths may be made without reference to modern building advice – old bricks, tiles or stone slabs laid onto bare earth instead of a bed of concrete or sand, to achieve a charmingly authentic unevenness. And old plant containers with cracks, chips, or corners missing look perfectly at home in a cottage garden – a good location, perhaps, for a group of sedums and sempervivums.

COTTAGE TOPIARY

Although true topiary came not from cottage gardens but from those of the wealthy classes, it is fast becoming a fashionable cottage-garden feature today. Many of the old cottage gardens however contained trimmed trees and shrubs of various sorts. A holly tree growing up through the hedge would often have been clipped into a 'lollipop' shape. And plants such as winter jasmine were trimmed neatly to form a porch round the front door, supported by a few poles or a latticework structure.

Nowadays, our porches are usually more permanently built and completely enclosed, but even so they can be clad with trimmed plants. A few people still have a clipped holly, but box is now more commonly seen as a shaped specimen in a cottage garden. The dwarf variety (*Buxus sempervirens* 'Suffruticosa') makes a neat, naturally low-growing edging for a formal or semi-formal bed, and is also useful for creating the pattern of a knot garden. *Santolina* or lavender give a slightly less formal finish. The larger-growing box, yew, or fast-growing *Lonicera nitida*, can be trimmed into topiary shapes – such as peacocks, teapots, spirals or pyramids – although establishing these shapes is a rather specialized art. Other sorts of trees can also be successfully trimmed into shapes. At Barnsley House in Gloucestershire, for instance, there is a row of lollipop-trimmed hawthorn trees at one end of the ornamental vegetable garden, and running along one side is an evergreen hedge whose top has been clipped into 'battlements'.

BELOW LEFT
Dahlias planted in a formal garden in Hampshire, with neatly clipped box hedges outlining the straight-edged beds. A planted urn acts as the focal point at the centre of the pattern of beds.

BELOW RIGHT
A very formal feature does not, surprisingly, look at all out of place in the informal surroundings of a cottage garden. Here a topiary box tree makes a stunning contrast with the house and garden. And although such complicated topiary takes more trimming than a simple shape or a low hedge, you can get away with cutting box once a year in late summer. Hand shears are essential – electric hedgetrimmers do not give you enough fine control.

A true wild garden in Suffolk demonstrates the considerable charm that this kind of planting can offer. The plants grown are a mixture of rather invasive wild countryside flowers, like pink campion, and rampant self-seeders like honesty. Yet among them you will find the occasional 'treasure', like the *Allium bulgaricum* just in front of the *Garrya elliptica* tree. Natural though it looks, the wild garden is carefully contained in one area – in the background you can just make out the informal planting of old roses and shrubs that make up the garden beyond.

A colourful border packed with old-fashioned flowers complements the wisteria-clad walls of this old cottage in Somerset. Oriental poppies, aquilegia, roses, *Nepeta*, *Gladiolus communis byzantinus*, and marguerites (*Argyranthemum*) make a bold splash of early summer colour in the traditional cottage style.

WILD FLOWERS

It would be difficult to create a convincing cottage garden without including at least a few native wild flowers, trees or shrubs, or their immediate descendants. Wild flowers and native species of shrub, such as the guelder rose (*Viburnum opulus*), can be included in an informal border along with modern hybrids and cultivars, or used to create a wild garden which recreates the natural look of the countryside. A small lightly wooded area makes an attractive wild garden and can look lovely naturalized with bluebells, primroses and spring bulbs. A natural-looking pond makes a good setting for damp-loving wild plants such as marsh marigold and reedmace.

But even in a small garden where there is not room for a proper wild area, you can allow wild flowers to intrude into grass, or include old-fashioned flowers in your borders, such as double primroses and lady's smock, bachelor's buttons (the double-flowered forms of several native *Ranunculus* species), and ornamental celandines such as 'Brazen Hussy' that are the direct descendants of wild species. Nowadays all of these plants can be obtained from nurseries in cultivated form either as growing plants or as seed or bulbs, and should *not* be dug up from the wild.

OLD-FASHIONED FLOWERS

The old-fashioned flowers frequently have assets their modern counterparts have lost – a powerful scent, unusual colours or markings, or a completely different flower shape. And there is now quite a movement to preserve and reintroduce these old cultivars, which have often been superseded by modern kinds with larger flowers, brighter colours and longer flowering seasons. The 'disadvantages' many modern nurserymen perceive in the old varieties can be turned to advantage in the right sort of garden. Old-fashioned roses and pinks, for instance, are notorious for their short flowering season – but this trait means that, like the early cottagers, you can enjoy a constantly changing scene, with each flower having its own particular season of interest. Also, you will be able to grow a greater variety of flowers in the same space, so your garden will look more interesting, not less so.

Many old-fashioned flowers have much better scent than their modern counterparts – roses, pinks, old-fashioned *Nicotiana* and sweet peas are good examples. And their shapes are more varied – for example among the old varieties of roses there are quartered flowers, Moss roses with shaggy green calyces and Centifolia roses with hundreds of frilly petals, to name but a few. Old-fashioned flowers may also come in colours or patterns that are no longer common – striped flowers were extremely popular several centuries ago, and striped roses such as 'Variegata di Bologna' and rosa mundi help give a garden an old-fashioned look for this reason.

The Thatched Cottage, Buckinghamshire, is thought to date back to medieval times. It is tiny, only one storey high, with a deep, overhanging thatched roof. An old perpetual sweet pea grows on the south-facing front of the cottage; this is one of the few remaining plants from the original overgrown garden, which the present owners completely replanned and replanted.

An Old-Fashioned Cottage Garden

The Thatched Cottage, near Aylesbury in Buckinghamshire, dates back to medieval times, and the owners set out to create a garden that was in keeping with the character of their home. They began to stock the garden several years before old-fashioned flowers and plants had the popularity they now enjoy, so the job entailed travelling the country hunting out scarce old varieties from remote nurseries and cottage gardens. So successful have they been that their garden is a plant-lover's paradise, and they have started their own nursery specializing in old-fashioned rarities.

The garden was created in much the same way as the early cottage gardens were – bit by bit. Before starting work the owners laid down a few 'ground rules' for creating an old-fashioned effect. They decided to make a lot of small flowerbeds, rather than a few large ones and not to mix shrubs and flowers together in the same bed. The beds now contain perennial flowers, while trees and shrubs are planted mainly round the edge of the garden.

The plants would include many herbs grown for scent and to attract bees into the garden. Although not all the flowers are genuinely old fashioned – modern plants are included if they look right – conifers and heathers have been excluded as being inappropriate for a cottage garden. They also

The long narrow bed that runs along the front of The Thatched Cottage is backed by a low lavender hedge that spills over onto the path behind it. The bed contains an extravagant mixture of sun-loving plants chosen for scent, and to attract bees and butterflies, as well as for their old-fashioned look. The unusually deep thatch deflects rain water well away from the cottage walls, so the plants growing against the cottage are prone to dry out in summer and have to be kept watered. The golden variegated jasmine in the flowerpot in the foreground is trained up onto the roof every summer, where it makes a fine contrast with the dark thatch.

The path disappears round the corner of The Thatched Cottage through a rose-and-honeysuckle-covered arch into the back garden. Looking back towards the front garden, straight ahead on the far side of the arch is a border planned for spring interest. This leads gradually on to a wild area, complete with wild flowers, pond, hedgehogs and frogs. The owners have taken pains to encourage wildlife to visit their garden – although the original occupants of their ancient cottage may not have been as keen to provide a home for animals and insects.

ABOVE
To the left of the rose arch, a selection of shade-loving cottage-garden plants have been planted round the back of the house, which, facing north, is permanently in shadow. In the foreground is one of the garden's main features – a large topiary box tree. When the present owners took over the garden this was a neglected tangle of branches, and its present bowler-hat form was the easiest shape to carve from the mass of overgrown shoots. Its curves are reflected in the easy bends of the nearby flowerbeds.

RIGHT
Towards the end of the back garden, beds of tall perennial flowers – including the very striking and unusual *Achillea grandifolia* – stand out well against the hedge in the background. Although this looks like a genuine, old country hedge, it was in fact planted by the present owners, in traditional style, using a mixture of species such as blackthorn, beech, hornbeam, cherry plum, hawthorn and wych elm. Besides looking appropriate it provides a good habitat for birds. The building on the right is modern, but has been thoughtfully designed to blend into the garden, and provides architectural interest.

The old rose 'Maiden's Blush' and frothy cream *Aruncus* flowers, together with variegated and gold foliage and silver-dollar-shaped honesty seedheads, make a muted picture at the back of The Thatched Cottage. Oriental poppies are generally considered to be difficult flowers to place in a garden, but here their vivid vermilion provides just the right splash of colour to turn an interesting corner into one that is really arresting.

aimed for a traditional mixed colour scheme, rather than special colour groupings, but clashing colours have been avoided. And to help the garden merge into the surrounding countryside, a small wild area planted with native flowers and shrubs with a small natural pond for the frogs, has been left in front of the cottage. Although small, the garden has been planned so that it is not entirely visible from the house, in order to preserve the element of surprise. It has been planted to retain interest – rather than colour – all the year round.

The cottage is a low, narrow single-storey thatched building. On its front wall grows an old perennial sweet pea, one of the few original plants that still remains in the garden. All along the front of the cottage, which faces south, is a narrow flowerbed backed by an informal lavender hedge and densely packed with an enormous mixture of old-fashioned plants chosen for their scent and to attract bees and butterflies close to the cottage. In this border, height is an important consideration – the plants need to be reasonably low so as not to obscure the tiny, low windows of the cottage.

Separating the border from the front of the cottage is a narrow stone-paved path which leads from the road through a gate at the side of the cottage, past the front door, through a rustic archway planted with roses and honeysuckle and round into the back garden. Here, parts of the paving are noticeably older than the rest; large cobblestones sunk into the earth once formed the original path to the cottage and several were uncovered when the present owners were redesigning the garden. Now, thoughtfully incorporated into the scheme, they make a fascinating period feature.

Another old feature is the box tree trimmed into a topiary shape, best described as a bowler hat. When the present owners took over the garden, the box was very overgrown and its present shape was chosen as being most closely suggested by the framework of branches, so trimming it was comparatively easy.

The back of the house, which faces north and never gets the sun, has been planted with shade-loving plants such as foxgloves, hellebores, geraniums and lily-of-the-valley. Paths wind between the many smallish beds in the back garden, where taller herbs and flowers grow. In the centre, behind the herb bed, a wooden seat nestles beneath a bower clad with wisteria, clematis and roses, providing a secluded place to sit screened from the lane behind. There is no vegetable plot, but a few apple trees have been planted at either end of the garden, and tucked into a corner behind the shed are gooseberry, blackberry and currant bushes.

At the end of the back garden is an outbuilding which was added by the present owners, who use it as an office for their nursery business. Although new, it has been designed to blend sympathetically with the garden and it helps provide a focal point and a variation in background to the mixed hedge of native trees and shrubs planted round the perimeter.

7

Traditional Cottage Flowers

Which flowers should you include in a cottage garden? Many people happily include any flowers that look 'cottagey', regardless of their age or origins. But for others, greater authenticity is important. The following is a short selection of some of the most interesting and useful of the authentic cottage-garden flowers, not including herbs, fruit and vegetables, and roses, which have already been dealt with at length in previous chapters of this book.

Hollyhocks are the hallmark of an authentic cottage garden. In the past the same clump would have been left to grow larger and larger each year.

ALCHEMILLA

Alchemilla mollis, Lady's mantle. Low-growing herbaceous plant with neat rounded leaves patterned with pleats. Flowers from mid to late summer in loose sprays of lime green to sulphur yellow, which seem to drift above the canopy of leaves like foam. Good for cutting. Plants self-seed readily given suitable conditions. Superb ground-cover plants for sun or shade.

AQUILEGIA

Aquilegia vulgaris, granny's bonnets, columbine. Delicate foliage; nodding spurred flowers produced on 2 ft (60 cm) stems in a range of pinks, blues, mauves and creams, including

bicolours and unusual double forms, throughout late spring and early summer just before the roses start. Look beautiful when allowed to push up through shrubs, associating well with bluebells. Self-seed freely; propagate named varieties by division in autumn. Sun or shade.

ASTRANTIA

Masterwort, Hattie's pincushion. Charming old-fashioned herbaceous plants, about 18 in (45 cm) with low-growing leaves, which flower from mid to late summer, producing many smallish button-like flowers each surrounded by a shaggy collar of bracts of similar colour. Good for cutting, and much loved by flower arrangers. Varieties: *A. maxima*, pale pink flowers; *A. major rubra*, red flowers; *A. major* 'Shaggy', pink buds and greenish white flowers; *A. major* 'Sunningdale Variegated', pinkish green flowers and cream and lime variegated leaves. Propagate from seed, or by dividing large clumps up in early spring or autumn. Sun or partial shade.

AURICULA

Primula auricula, bear's ears, mountain cowslips. Small low-growing clumps of shiny green ovate leaves, covered with a sprinkling of whitish 'farina' in some varieties. The flowers appear in clusters on short stalks in late spring. Many varieties have attractive 'eyes' in the centre of the flowers. A good selection of very old varieties are still available. Border and alpine auriculas are the best for garden cultivation and most easily obtained. Show auriculas, which have circles of 'paste' in the centre of their flowers and green, grey or white 'paste' edgings to the petals, are scarce treasures that have to be grown under glass to protect the flowers. Propagate by detaching offsets, which are often already partly rooted, shortly after flowering is over. Sun or partial shade.

BACHELOR'S BUTTONS

The name 'bachelor's buttons' seems to have been given to more than one plant of the *Ranunculus* tribe, all of which were old cottage-garden favourites. These include *R. aconitifolius* 'Flore Pleno' (white bachelor's buttons), a 2 ft (60 cm) buttercup-like plant with small white double button flowers, also called fair maids of France, or, confusingly fair maids of Kent, which flowers in early summer; also the double version of our native meadow buttercup, *R. acris* 'Flore Pleno', which has tight yellow button-like flowers on 3 ft (1 m) stems from mid to late summer; and the double creeping buttercup, *R. repens pleniflorus*. Propagate by dividing up clumps in early spring, or from seed. Requires moist soil, sun or partial shade.

CATMINT

Nepeta × faassenii. Slightly invasive plants with soft silvery grey leaves and lavender flowers from midsummer to autumn. *N.*

'Six Hills Giant' grows 2 ft (60 cm) tall and is a tough plant that looks well growing among old-fashioned roses. The smaller *N. mussinii* is sprawling and low-growing, ideal for softening the edges of a border or path. Propagate by cuttings in summer. Warm dry sunny site.

CHAMOMILE

Chamaemelum nobile. A herb with pretty bright-green ferny foliage and single 6 in (15 cm) daisy-like flowers with white petals and a yellow boss in the centre, throughout the summer. Flowers used to be infused to make a rinse for fair hair, and a tea said to aid insomnia. A double-flowered version, 'Flore Pleno', is rather more choice and needs a very well-drained soil. Propagation by seed, division or cuttings. Sunny site.

CLEMATIS

The original clematis of old cottage gardens was the wild traveller's joy, *Clematis vitalba*, which has insignificant flowers

and fluffy seedheads. Nowadays a vast range of species and large-flowered hybrid clematis are readily available, and it is possible to choose a selection of plants to provide flowers or fluffy seedheads through most of the season. In spring, *C. alpina* and *C. montana* cultivars, followed by large-flowered hybrids such as *C. × jackmanii*, 'Bee's Jubilee', 'Ville de Lyon', 'Rouge Cardinal', etc., which flower from midsummer onwards. Late-flowering species, such as *C. tangutica*, with nodding yellow flowers, and improved forms such as *C. orientalis* 'Bill Macken-zie', have very different flowers to the hybrids and are followed by dense silky seedheads. A particularly charming late-flowering species is the old-fashioned, double flowered *C.v.* 'Purpurea Plena Elegans', which has faded grey-violet flowers.

Plant clematis with their roots in the shade of other plants, but where their tops can grow into sun – on trellis on walls, over arches, and up through trees, shrubs and climbing roses. Propagation at home is not easy.

CROWN IMPERIAL

Fritillaria imperialis. Often grown in rows in old cottage gardens; the best-known kind has reddish orange flowers, through there are also – now rare – yellow-flowered and even variegated-leaved crown imperials. The bell-like flowers, which hang in a bunch beneath a tuft of leaves on 2 ft 6 in (75 cm) stems, appear in late spring. Plant with a handful of gritty sand under the bulbs to prevent rotting. Sun or partial shade.

DAISY

Bellis perennis. Similar to the common daisies, but with double flowers on 6 in (15 cm) stems. Were used for edging paths in old cottage gardens, or grown with other plants near the front of a border. They can also be used for spring and summer bedding – the plants begin flowering in spring and remain in bloom continuously until late summer. Some old named varieties such as 'Dresden China' (terracotta pink) are still available. The curious 'hen and chickens' daisy, *B. perennis* 'Prolifera', has double daisy flowers surrounded by dangling clusters of smaller flowers attached to the main head by short strands. This would have been grown in a border, but was often used as a pot plant on cottage windowsills. Divide up clumps in autumn. Sunny site.

EUPHORBIA

Spurge. Not really traditional old cottage-garden plants, euphorbias nevertheless look very much at home in cottage

gardens. They have glaucous leaves and insignificant flowers surrounded by clusters of green or yellow bracts. Several species and cultivars are readily available: *E. characias wulfenii* grows 3 ft (1 m) high with large lime-green heads; 'Lambrook Gold' is a butter-yellow selection of it – both are in great demand from flower arrangers; *E. griffithii* 'Fireglow' has unusual orange bracts. Propagate named varieties by cuttings. All flower in late spring and early summer, and need fairly well-drained soil in sun or partial shade.

FOXGLOVE

Digitalis purpurea. Wild foxgloves would have seeded themselves into cottage gardens from the surrounding countryside. Nowadays you only need to introduce plants once or twice to

get a good colony growing this way. The 4 ft (1.2 m), purple-flowered plants will self-seed almost anywhere, but look best allowed to naturalize in light woodland or in a wildish border among trees. Cultivated varieties come in pink, mauve, cream or apricot colours. Pull up seedlings that appear where you don't want them rather than transplanting them elsewhere.

FUCHSIA

Although cottage gardeners in the past would not have had the facilities to keep 'normal' fuchsias through the winter, they

grew a few of the hardy kinds such as *F. magellanica*, which has drooping scarlet flowers on a 3–4 ft (1–1.2 m) shrubby plant. It is not fully hardy, and its roots need to be covered with a thick layer of ashes or peat every winter after the shoots are cut down to ground level. Propagation is easy from cuttings in late spring. Sun or partial shade.

GARDENER'S GARTERS

Phalaris arundinacea 'Picta', ribbon grass. An intriguingly named grass 2–3 ft (60 cm to 1 m) tall, its leaves variegated with longitudinal cream stripes. In late summer, ghostly white grassy seedheads seem to hover above the clumps. Spreads from rhizomous roots, and can be rather invasive. Thrives even in wet or clay soil. Propagate by division in spring. Sun or partial shade.

GERANIUM

Geranium species. Hardy geraniums (as distinct from the geraniums which should properly be called pelargoniums) are very popular cottage-garden plants. Many of the varieties we now enjoy are derived from the wild meadow cranesbills, and have the typical beak-like projections from their seedheads which give them their name. Most geraniums grow 1–2 ft (30–60 cm) high and make good ground cover under roses and shrubs, flowering through most of the summer, though some species do best on the rock garden. Most have single flowers but a few scarce varieties have very attractive double flowers. Different species are available with white, pink, blue, mauve or deep purple and even almost black flowers. Geraniums appreciate sun or partial shade. Propagation is by seed, basal cuttings or division in spring or autumn.

HELLEBORE

Helleborus species. Many have evergreen leaves and are valuable for their early spring flowers, which last well outdoors. Varieties: *H. niger* (the Christmas rose) has large open-faced white single flowers which, despite their name, usually flower after Christmas; *H. foetidus* has long drooping sprays of green bell-shaped flowers produced throughout early spring; *H. orientalis* has flowers similar to the Christmas rose but pink and spotted; *H. viridis* is a British native flower which has been cultivated in cottage gardens for very many years – it has blue-green flowers in early spring, and unlike the previous three is not evergreen. The 1–2 ft (30–60 cm) plants grow in sun or partial shade, and slowly form into clumps which can then be propagated by division.

HOLLYHOCK

Alcea rosea. No cottage is complete without a group of 6 ft (2 m) tall hollyhocks growing in front of a wall or by the door. Now that hollyhock rust is a problem these flowers are often treated as biennials, but they are true perennials and in the past a clump would have been left to increase and get taller year by year. Many named varieties of hollyhock were once available, but now a limited selection of single and double kinds in a variety of colours can be grown from seed, such as 'Chater's Double'. Sow in spring or early summer and transplant to their final position in autumn to flower the following year. Sun or partial shade.

IRIS

Flags. Blue flag irises would have grown in old cottage gardens, but now there are an enormous range of bearded irises available in a good range of colours – pink, orange, yellow, blue, mauve, violet, copper, and nearly black. They flower in midsummer and grow 3–4 ft (1–1.2 m) tall. Dwarf bearded irises are also available, growing only about 1 ft (30 cm) high, and flowering in early summer. Propagate by division a month after flowering is over. Sunny site.

LILY

Lily species such as *Lilium candidum*, *L. martagon* (pink turk's cap flowers) and *L. chalcedonicum* (orange turk's cap flowers) grew in early cottage gardens. The most commonly seen today is

L. candidum, the Madonna lily, which is probably one of the oldest cultivated plants. Its white flowers are heavily scented, growing on 4 ft (1.2 m) stems in midsummer. They were allowed to grow into large clumps in cottage gardens, since like many cottage-garden plants they dislike disturbance. Unlike most lilies, *L. candidum* should not be planted deeply; ideally the 'nose' of each bulb should just be visible above the soil surface. It likes a chalky soil with plenty of organic matter, and a sunny spot among other plants which will shade its roots. Nowadays a great number of large-flowered hybrid lilies are available with huge trumpet-shaped flowers in yellow, red, pink, white and orange shades, some scented and some not. Plant in spring as soon as bulbs are available in good well-drained soil, with the roots in the shade of other plants but where the tops can grow up into sun.

LOOSESTRIFE

Lysimachia punctata, yellow willow herb, yellow loosestrife. Slightly invasive perennial plants with small oval leaves and

LUNGWORT

Pulmonaria species. Once thought to cure lung complaints, these small plants are useful for ground cover, growing almost anywhere in sun or shade. Their large spotted leaves and clusters of pink and blue bell-shaped flowers, similar to those of their relative borage, appear in early spring when there is little else out. *P. rubra* has the earliest flowers, which are red, but its leaves are not spotted. *P. saccharata* 'Mrs Moon' is a specially good form with heavily spotted leaves and pink and blue flowers. Plant pulmonaria among wildflowers, or in a border where later plants can grow up through the foliage. Propagate by division in autumn.

LUPIN

Lupinus cultivars. It was not till the early 1930s that the famous Russell strain was produced, which is the forerunner of today's large multicoloured affairs. The lupin's 3 ft (1 m) flower spikes appear in midsummer, and it may produce a second flush if you cut the old flower stems down to the base of the plants as soon as they are over. Propagate by cuttings in spring or by dividing clumps in spring or autumn. There is also a tree lupin, *L. arboreus*, with yellow flowers on 2–4 ft (60 cm to 1.2 m) spikes. Grow both in sun.

MYRTLE

Myrtus communis. Slightly tender, 3 ft (1 m) high evergreen shrub with dark green, shiny leaves, and large, heavily scented white flowers in midsummer, which was commonly grown just outside the front door of old cottages. Traditionally used in wedding bouquets, it was once customary for a bridesmaid to plant a slip of myrtle taken from the bride's bouquet, and if it rooted she could expect to marry shortly. Sunny sheltered spot.

NARCISSUS

Daffodils and narcissi have been cottage-garden flowers since way back – the old, scented, pheasant's eye (*N. poeticus recurvus*) is one of the original favourites. They look good planted in drifts in grass, especially under apple trees, on a grassy bank or in a flower lawn. They can be a problem in flowerbeds, having a lot of foliage which does not die down for several months after flowering. Miniature species such as *NN. cyclamineus*, *bulbo-codium* and *triandrus* and varieties derived from them such as 'February Gold' and 'Jack Snipe', are easier to manage in borders as they have less foliage. Plant bulbs in autumn and leave undisturbed to form clumps. Propagate by dividing clumps when foliage dies down after flowering.

NASTURTIUM

Tropaeolum majus, great Indian cress. Ideal cottage garden flowers, being annuals that seed themselves, given reasonably favourable conditions. A situation with plenty of sun suits them perfectly, especially if the soil is rather poor. They'll scramble over fences, up netting or cover nearby shrubs in a mass of orange trumpet flowers and circular leaves all summer long. You can also train them over rustic arches. The old double nasturtium 'Hermine Grashof' still exists, though it is very scarce; it is more compact than the trailing kind, and has pinky-orange flowers. It does not produce seed and must be propagated from cuttings – keep a few on a windowsill or in the greenhouse as plants do not survive the winter outside. Poor, dryish soil and plenty of sun.

PANSY

Viola cultivars. Originally raised from selections of wild heartsease, *V. tricolor*, in the early 1800s, pansies quickly became collector's plants, specially bred for exhibition with flowers in one, two or three colours, and even with striped petals. Further crossbreeding produced plants suitable for general garden cultivation. Modern pansies are grown from seed and treated as annuals, they will also self-seed themselves freely; old named varieties of viola, such as 'Jackanapes', have to be grown from cuttings as seed cannot be guaranteed to come true to type. Cuttings should be taken in mid to late summer. Partial shade.

PEONY

Paeonia officinalis and its varieties. The old cottage peony starts flowering in early summer, slightly earlier than the Chinese peonies normally grown nowadays, which flower in midsummer. The flowers of *P. officinalis* varieties resemble overblown cabbage roses, and last longer than those of Chinese peonies; the plants are more robust too, growing $2\frac{1}{2}$ ft (75 cm) high with handsome foliage that looks good all summer. Varieties: 'Alba Plena', double white; 'Rubra Plena', double red; 'Rosea Plena', double pink. Large clumps can be propagated by division in early autumn, though generally peonies dislike disturbance. Sun or partial shade.

PERENNIAL SWEET PEA

Lathyrus latifolius. Similar to annual sweet peas, but with no scent and less fancy flowers, and do not need to be replanted each year. A favourite flower for covering walls or growing up through shrubs. Flowers throughout summer with small com-

pact bright magenta and pink blooms. Good for cutting. Produces a tangled mass of foliage and tendrils which are cut down at the end of each season when they start to dry out and turn brown. Propagate from seed. Sunny site.

PINKS

Dianthus cultivars, gillyflower. Early clove-scented pinks were grown in the grounds of inns and used in mulled wine, hence the common name of 'sops-in wine'. They enjoyed a surge of popularity when the weavers of Paisley in Scotland bred laced pinks with intricately patterned petals as show plants. Since then pinks of all sorts – single, double, fringed – have been popular as cottage-garden plants, growing 6–8 in (15–20 cm) tall, and now some of the old varieties have been rescued and are once again available from specialist nurseries. Varieties: 'Dad's Favourite', eighteenth-century laced pink with maroon-red lacing on white petals; 'Queen of Sheba', known to have existed in the seventeenth century, has single flowers with heavily feathered white markings on magenta petals; 'Bat's Double Red', double red with blue-grey foliage, dating back to early 1700s; 'Bridal Veil', double white with pink centre and silvery leaves, again dating back to 1700s. Grow in freely drained, slightly chalky soil and a sunny situation; propagate from cuttings in late summer.

POLYANTHUS

Polyanthus are thought to have originated from hybrids between common primroses, cowslips and a red primrose – they look more like cowslips, with a bunch of flowers on top of each 6–8 in (15–20 cm) stem. The early polyanthus were all red, but in 1710 a form with a distinctive gold edging appeared

– this was the forerunner of the popular gold-laced polyanthus. Many named varieties once existed, grown predominately by Yorkshire weavers who cultivated them for show. Gold-laced polyanthus can still be obtained but not under individual names; old silver-laced polyanthus can also sometimes be found. Modern seed strains of both exist, and of course a huge range of brightly coloured modern polyanthus are readily obtainable. Grow any polyanthus in sun or partial shade, on well-manured ground and propagate them by division in midsummer after flowering is finished.

POPPY

The wild opium poppy, *Papaver somniferum* – $2\frac{1}{2}$ ft (75 cm) tall hardy annual with large flowers and glaucous leaves – and the common cornfield poppy, *P. rhoeas* – small fragile bright-red flowers on hairy 10–12 in (25–30 cm) stems – would have arrived naturally in old cottage gardens every time the wind blew a fresh crop of seed in from the surrounding fields. However Oriental poppies, *P. orientale* – huge herbaceous plants with bright-coloured flowers – are more 'official' tenants

of modern cottage gardens, and many comparatively recent cultivars of annual and biennial poppies are grown both for their flowers and for their pepper-pot seedheads, which make good indoor winter decorations. Grow annual and biennial poppies from seed sown in spring or summer, on the spot as seedlings do not transplant well, and propagate Oriental poppies by dividing clumps in autumn or spring. Grow in sunny well drained soil.

PRIMROSE

Today cultivated primroses come in a huge range of colours, growing about 4 in (10 cm) high, but the original wild yellow *Primula vulgaris* was dug up from the fields and transplanted into cottage gardens. Double primroses, and different colours appeared later, and many of the old named varieties are still obtainable from specialist nurseries. The old doubles are often not easy to grow, however, 'Marie Crousse' – large double mauve flowers with silver edges to the petals, and *P. vulgaris* 'Lilacina Plena' – double lilac flowers, commonly known as Quaker's bonnet, are both quite easy. There is also said to have been a double green form. Specially fascinating are the hose-in-hose primroses, which look as if two primrose flowers are growing one inside the other, and Jack-in-the-green primroses, which have single flowers, each surrounded by a ruff of green leaves. Both are old-fashioned favourites which have recently become available again from specialists. Grow in moist, slightly shady places in well-manured soil, and propagate by division in summer, after flowering is over.

SALVIA

Sage. The early cottagers would have grown only the herb sage, *S. officinalis*, but nowadays many of the hardy herbaceous salvias find themselves at home in a cottage-garden border. Of the many kinds available *S. × superba* is one of the most useful as its tall upright flower spikes contrast well with the shapes of other border flowers. They also look good planted under roses, where the lavender-blue spikes push up between the branches and appear among the rose flowers. Plants grow 3 ft (1 m) tall, though a shorter form, 'East Friesland', is also available. Both flower from midsummer to early autumn. Plant in fairly well-drained soil in sun or very slight shade. Propagate by cuttings or division in spring.

SEMPERVIVUM

Houseleek. These small clusters of spiky succulent bodies are often grown in containers, between cracks in paving or even – in the West Country – on house roofs (because they were reputed to ward off lightning strikes). Houseleeks grow in any well-drained soil, and being shallow-rooted can gain a foot hold where there is very little soil at all. The plants have strange 1 in (2.5 cm) pillars of pink flowers in late spring. Propagation is easy by detaching offsets, which are normally already rooted, and potting or replanting them in summer.

SNOWDROP

Galanthus nivalis. One of the earliest-flowering spring bulbs, snowdrops are found in most cottage gardens. New plants are best established by dividing up large old clumps after flowering but while the leaves are still green; dry bulbs often do not survive or are slow to start growing away. Once planted, leave the clumps undisturbed. Snowdrops will grow well even in heavy shade and their small drooping white single or double flowers look attractive when they are naturalized in grass or round trees or shrubs, or planted in groups near a front door.

SYMPHYTUM

Symphytum grandiflorum, cherubim and seraphim. A real old cottage-garden plant, and specially valuable as it is one of the first to flower in the new year. It is one of the comfrey family, $2\frac{1}{2}$–3 ft (75 cm to 1 m) tall, with rough evergreen leaves and clusters of cream bell-shaped flowers with pale cinnamon shading towards the tips. Grows in most soils, and is easily propagated by division during the late spring or summer.

VIOLET

Viola odorata. Single violets, descended from wild violets, but in a larger range of colours – white, pale blue, pink or mauve – make good ground cover under hedges and in shady areas beneath other plants. Left to their own devices they spread slowly, and seed themselves. The larger, heavily scented, double Parma violets may sometimes have come the cottager's way, but were rather treasured and temperamental cultivars that would have been grown by gardeners at 'the big house' for cutting. They are now very rarely found, and not easy to keep.

WALLFLOWER

Cheiranthus cheiri. Wallflowers self-seeded themselves freely in old cottage gardens; their name is derived from their habit of settling themselves into the mortar of old walls. Although we now grow these glowing, velvety flowers from seed and treat them as annuals, they are in fact perennials and would have been left in old cottage gardens from one year to the next. Sow seed in mid to late summer and plant out in the autumn to flower the following spring. They grow 18 in (45 cm) tall. Several fascinating double wallflowers were available – which had to be grown from cuttings as they did not produce seed – including double red, yellow, black and even green, though now only the double red, 'Bloody Warrior', and the double yellow, 'Harpur Crewe', are available.

WISTERIA

Wisteria sinensis. Probably not so much grown in very old cottage gardens as it is now. Wisteria are very large and vigorous climbers that need space to develop and time to flower. Plants may not start flowering until they are 6 to 8 years old and need proper pruning to keep them within bounds and to encourage flowering instead of thickets of vegetative growth. Plant wisterias on a sunny wall or if you have room and wish to avoid pruning entirely, up through large trees.

8

Effect and Ornament

The most successful cottage gardens don't rely solely on plants for their effect. Although plants are undoubtedly the main consideration, various other elements also play an important part. Paths, paving, walls, seats, plant containers and sundials are just some of the many 'architectural' elements that go to make up cottage gardens. These 'non plant' features provide a vital contrast in colour and texture to surrounding flowers and foliage; arches and walls add height to an otherwise flat garden, besides creating places for climbing plants to grow, while steps contribute further to the feeling of changing levels. One very underrated if somewhat intangible 'element' is that of curiosity; the garden should never be too predictable.

The garden of Knapp Lane Farmhouse, Somerset, has been developed into a series of miniature gardens. Each 'plot' has a character of its own that is often centred around an inanimate object, such as this seakale forcing pot, which makes a pleasing contrast to the surrounding flowers and foliage. As you walk round the garden, you find several such feature areas, linked together by narrow winding paths.

PATHS AND STEPS

These are the most functional of the 'elements'. In the very early days of cottages, earth paths would have 'happened' wherever the occupants needed to walk. In time, cinders from the fire would have been spread over muddy patches, until eventually a proper path was formed. Traditionally there would have been a straight path from the garden gate to the front door. Other paths would have led round to the back of the cottage, strategically placed to enable the cottager to gather herbs and vegetables or visit the privy in comparative comfort even in wet weather. These provided the only durable footing through 'wall to wall' planting or long, wet, rough grass.

Today, too, it's a good idea to plan your main pathways so

that they take you where you want to go – to the garage, shed, washing line or dustbins – and as efficiently as possible. Functional paths do not need to run in a completely straight line, they can meander a little, but if they divert from their true direction too much, short cuts will be taken that in time will wear 'unofficial' paths into lawn, flower beds or even through low hedges, spoiling the look of the garden. These functional paths can nevertheless be interesting to look at, constructed of old bricks laid in herringbone patterns (buy them secondhand from builders' yards that specialize in reclaiming old materials), flat stones attractively interplanted with low, scented thymes, or gravel with self-seeded plants allowed to ramble at will. You can also soften the hard lines of functional paths with sprawling plants such as *Erysimum* spilling over the edges.

Non-functional paths are designed to let you enjoy rambling round the garden looking at plants; they also play an important design role by linking different parts of the garden together. In some gardens, paths merely provide an alternative to walking on grass, but many gardeners like to include an area which is more like the original cottage gardens in character – where there is no grass at all, just plants with paths winding through them.

Like paths, steps play a dual role in a garden. On a sloping site, steps are by far the most practical way of walking from one level to another – except with a wheelbarrow, and from a design point of view they make a definite distinction between the levels. On a flat site, the illusion of a change in levels – however slight – is worth the effort involved in creating it. A couple of shallow steps recessed into the ground may not actually take you anywhere, but the eye is nevertheless tricked into thinking they do. Regardless of whether they fulfil a real function or not, steps provide an opportunity for adding a hard surface somewhere that needs a contrast to surrounding plant material, whether that may be lawn, or a natural gap between borders. Steps also play a useful role in preparing the onlooker for a change of scene beyond, and act as an introduction to a new part of the garden. They may be formal – made of stone or concrete paving slabs, or less formal – made of gravel or bark chippings infilled between timber risers.

This tiny Buckinghamshire garden is landscaped on three levels, the top storey of which is reached by several series of steps. To make the best use of space, besides adding all-year-round colour, the risers of this flight have been picked out with the yellow ivy 'Buttercup', and a cream and green variegated kind. Surrounding plants are encouraged to spill over the edges of the steps to soften the hard lines.

A tripod of rustic poles supports a golden hop (*Humulus lupulus aureus*) in a garden in Somerset. Growing a climber up supporting poles is one of the quickest ways of adding height to a border without waiting for shrubs to grow up, and the resulting plant 'pillar' is easily accessible for trimming or pruning.

Many real old cottage gardens contained a bower – somewhere partially enclosed and covered with climbers to sit in comfort after a hard day's work in the fields. In this Oxfordshire cottage vegetable patch, a seat with a surround of rustic hurdles matching the adjacent fence fulfils the same function.

POLES AND ARCHES

Another way of creating the illusion of changing levels in a flat garden is to add height. By growing climbing plants, such as clematis, honeysuckle or roses, up poles you can give height to a border, either in isolated spots by growing one or two plants up a vertical pole, or by joining a series of poles together to form a continuous raised backdrop to a long border. Arches not only add height to a flat area, they also form a very attractive 'doorway' through into another part of the garden. Sited with care, an archway covered in climbing plants becomes the frame for a picture formed by the garden beyond. All sorts of material can be used to make arches and raised frameworks to grow plants on, but the most popular in cottage gardens are rustic poles. These can usually be bought quite cheaply, but if the garden happens to include a few hazel, willow or poplar trees in the hedge or in a belt of woodland, then these may be coppiced to provide a regular supply of poles. Alternatively, sawn and treated 3 × 1 in (8 × 2.5 cm) timber can be used. However, since the structure will very quickly be covered by climbing plants, it won't matter too much if the supporting framework is made from modern plastic-covered wire mesh or other similar material. The uprights for poles and arches can simply be dug into the soil, or set in concrete for a more permanent structure.

SEATS AND BOWERS

Seats, in a cottage garden, are more than just somewhere to sit – they are an integral part of the landscape. And while modern garden furniture is inexpensive and functional, it just doesn't look 'right', besides needing to be put away in winter, which means having a shed or space in the garage to store it. Most cottage gardeners prefer wooden benches that look the part, and can be left out of doors all the year round. Some like to have a group of chairs, or a bench and a table, permanently placed in a favourite spot close to the house, where they can escape

outdoors at every opportunity. A paved area is usually chosen for placing permanent seating so there is no need to move everything each time the lawn needs mowing. But as well as having a sitting-out area, many cottage gardens also include rustic wooden benches as a focal point at the end of paths, or in cosy niches framed by plants. Such places are chosen with great consideration, both for the view of the seat from the garden, and the view of the garden from the seat. And even though these secondary seats are not located for regular sitting, they undoubtedly provide pleasant 'pausing points' on a gentle stroll round the garden.

Many early cottage gardens would have had an arbour or bower – a structure of rustic poles or interwoven withies over which grew roses and climbing plants, which provided the cottager with somewhere secluded to sit at the end of the day's work, with a bit of protection from the wind. Although you rarely see these delightful rural 'buildings' any longer, a few cottage gardeners are beginning to appreciate their value. They can easily be made from willow prunings, woven hurdles, poles, or even sawn timber, with a slat, pole or wire netting 'roof', planted over with a mixture of climbing roses, honeysuckle and clematis.

Water features can be a lot of effort to maintain. The owner of Knapp Lane Farmhouse, Somerset, has added a suggestion of water without the work by reconstructing an old wellhead. Like many old cottages, this one has a real well in the garden, but for safety the original shaft is kept covered and the ornamental 'fake' seen here forms the centre of one of several attractive 'miniature' gardens.

GARDEN ORNAMENTS

Garden ornaments cover a very wide range of objects, ranging from statues and sculptures, through wellheads, bird baths and sundials, to urns, Victorian forcing pots and so forth. In fact, one aspect of cottage gardening many people particularly enjoy is discovering unwanted objects and turning them into attractive additions to their garden. There are plenty of instances of old chimney pots, land drains, cartwheels, milk churns, and grindstones being rescued and used to good effect in cottage gardens. And although it seems unlikely that ornaments would have played much part in genuine old cottage gardens, modern occupants find them a very useful means of adding focal points to particular areas. Placed in the centre of a small and rather formal 'garden within a garden', or at the end of a vista, or just tucked in among plants, garden ornaments invite the eye to enjoy the view set before it.

Most cottage gardeners choose simple rustic ornaments, but at Thame Cottage, Oxfordshire, an elegant nymph is surrounded by flowers, her colour standing out well from the dark background.

Unlike permanent features, such as paths or paving, smaller ornaments give you some freedom to alter the look of the garden without the difficulty involved in moving plants. You can interchange them or move them around in order to shift emphasis to a different group of plants or to a different background. Larger and heavier garden ornaments tend to have permanent spaces allocated to them though; you might expect to find a statue tucked into a niche in a formal clipped hedge, or a sundial placed in the centre of a formal herb garden.

PLANT CONTAINERS

These are really just another sort of garden ornament, only here, instead of the ornament being the centre of attention, the focus is shared between container and plant. Where the container is large it may form a focal point of its own. But where containers are small or not specially outstanding, it is common to find several grouped together to make a pattern or to offer variations on a planting theme. For instance, a collection of clay terracotta pots of different sizes planted with scented plants, herbs or old-fashioned annuals makes a cohesive group by a back door, or standing on an area of paving or gravel.

Like other garden ornaments, plant containers frequently come into the category of *objets trouvés*. For example, a beautiful

The focal point of this living room in Somerset, is the view out over the garden through the french windows. A plain pot of marguerite standing on the tiled step acts as a gentle introduction to the cottage garden beyond. This is echoed further down the garden by other potted plants which guide the eye towards the centrepiece of the 'picture' – an old stone container filled with plants standing beside a staddle stone. The whole view is framed by surrounding shrubs, which give it a pleasantly enclosed, intimate feeling.

bronze bucket – with its bottom missing – found on a rubbish heap, and used, standing on a paving slab, as a plant container. Or the junction from an old section of guttering, fixed to the corner of a wall by the back door, and used to grow mint. Plenty of gardeners have taken advantage of local 'treasures' like old animal feeding troughs, stone sinks and Victorian chimney pots. Even now, cottage gardeners still tax their ingenuity for turning old junk into desirable plant containers by making synthetic stone containers from hypertufa. This is a mixture of peat, sand and cement that can be plastered on to a porcelain sink or over a shape made from several layers of wire netting. It can also be trowelled between two cardboard boxes placed one inside the other – a cheap and effective mould – to make a fake 'stone' sink. When dry, the container can be artificially aged by spraying it with liquid plant feed (or the real old country formula, watered-down cow manure), which encourages lichens and mosses to grow, giving an authentic finish that is surprisingly difficult to tell from real stone.

Natural water has been taken advantage of at Mill House, West Sussex, where the banks of the old mill stream have been landscaped with a mixture of bog and moisture-loving plants. Candelabra primulas and mimulus show up well against the foliage of ligularias that will flower later in the season. The far bank of the stream has been planted with many different ornamental willows, whose colourful stems provide winter interest.

A man-made pond at Ebbsworth Cottage, West Sussex, has been naturalized into its surroundings by a deep fringe of foliage. Waterside plants often have a relatively short flowering period, so choosing those with contrasting foliage helps to create all-season interest. Here, the pond water is circulated by a pump that feeds it back via a short artificial stream, which passes over a series of stones to produce the sound of running water. Nearby a rustic seat provides a quiet spot to sit and enjoy this tranquil environment.

WATER

Water is not a particularly traditional ingredient of cottage gardens, but it is one a lot of people like to incorporate nowadays – with good reason, since it gives a very relaxing atmosphere. It adds the extra dimensions of reflection and sound to a garden, as well as movement in the form of gently swaying reeds and darting dragonflies. It also provides an ideal habitat for moisture-loving plants that could not otherwise be accommodated.

The natural look is very definitely the one most modern cottage gardeners prefer when creating a water feature. Though a pond may have been artificially made, wild plants, or a judicious blend of wild and cultivated plants, with other features such as stepping stones, and surroundings of native shrubs and wild flowers give a feeling of naturalness. Some gardens, such as Mill House in West Sussex, are lucky enough to have natural water in the garden. Here, the original mill stream has been made into a feature of the garden by planting the banks thickly with bog plants. Nearby, a series of springs that erupt from the sloping lawns have been landscaped to form pools that are constantly fed by their own water supply.

Artificial water features can be created by a combination of excavation and butyl liners, as has been done at Ebbsworth Cottage, West Sussex. Both natural and man-made ponds take some effort to maintain as, unless it is kept moving, the water frequently goes green or develops excessive amounts of the thick algae called blanket weed. Although this sort of problem

may vanish with time, once the natural balance of the pond has been established, the most effective remedy is to build in a pump to circulate the water. (As a last resort, various chemicals are available that can be added to murky water to clear it). Incorporating a pump has the extra benefit that you can link up a series of small ponds with a small artificial stream to make a bigger feature. And it also enables you to run the circulated water over cobblestones or a small log to produce the pretty gurgling sounds so reminiscent of a real stream.

HEDGES AND TOPIARY

In the country, hedges are normally made of good stock-proof plants like hawthorn, or a mixture of shrubs such as wild rose, blackthorn and elder. Frequently, the clipped line of the hedge is broken by an occasional tree. But if you are planting a new boundary for a cottage garden or a dividing hedge within it, you may prefer something more decorative such as yew or box, or a flowering hedge of old-fashioned or species roses, which are pruned rather than clipped, or for a low hedge, rosemary, lavender or santolina. Alternatively, you might choose to have an informal screen of shrubs rather than a hedge. Ornamental willows with coloured stems such as *Salix violacea*, for instance, are particularly useful as windbreaks – the old shoots are pruned out at ground level in early spring each year to encourage vigorous new shoots with good colour. Or you could go for a mixture of flowering trees and shrubs chosen for colour throughout the season or, if you want to encourage wildlife, go for species bearing plenty of fruit, nuts, hips and berries – such as *Viburnum opulus*, *Rosa rugosa* 'Alba', *Corylus*, elder, hawthorn, or rowan.

But since cottage gardens are traditionally a blend of formal and informal plantings, it is quite common to find some hedges, trees and bushes clipped into shapes. Cottage-garden topiary can range from a simple row of 'battlements' along an evergreen hedge, to the highly trained and clipped shapes that are once again becoming popular. Trained yew or box trees can now be bought in a range of shapes – pyramids, spheres, etc., but it is not difficult to train your own, though obviously it can take time. For simple topiary, begin with small plants and clip them roughly into the required shape; continue to shape each year when the plants are trimmed in late summer. Complicated topiary shapes require wire frameworks to support the shoots – this is a tricky art that needs to be learnt properly.

Lonicera nitida is much faster growing than the popular yew and box but needs more frequent clipping to keep it in shape.

Once you get a taste for topiary, the possibilities are endless! Hedges can be clipped to resemble natural or unnatural shapes, and combined with formal features, such as flowerbeds outlined in miniature box hedges, create a garden which is both attractive and in character.

Santolina and the dwarf box (*Buxus sempervirens* 'Suffruticosa') make neat edgings for a formal bed, whether trained as a low hedge a few inches high or clipped into a row of spheres. Holly and hawthorn are more traditional plants for cottage topiary – allowed to grow up through country hedges and then clipped into 'lollipop' or umbrella shapes. They can also be grown as shaped specimen trees for the lawn.

LAWNS

Lawns would not have figured in early cottage gardens; space was needed for growing crops and herbs, and in any case, time was too precious to waste it cutting grass with a scythe. But today most gardens include at least a small patch of lawn. Many modern cottagers feel that a highly maintained, close-cropped lawn is out of place in a cottage garden, and prefer the more rural look of longer grass where perhaps wild flowers are encouraged to colonize. Grass seed mixtures that include wild flower seeds as well as lawn grasses are now available for growing wild flower lawns, or simply allow 'weeds' such as daisies, self-heal and speedwell to colonize an existing lawn. To encourage wild flowers, do not use weedkillers or fertilizers on a lawn. To maintain a real wild-flower lawn, cut the grass with a hand or motorized scythe in early spring and again after the flowers have set and scattered their seeds in late summer or early autumn. 'Weedy' lawns (which contain creeping wild flowers rather than tall upright species) should be mown regularly with the blades set high, and with the grass box on (as this impoverishes the turf and favours the flower species).

MYSTERY AND CURIOSITY

Mystery and curiosity are the most difficult 'elements' to plan into a cottage garden. But they are worth taking some trouble to include as they make the difference between a garden that is merely pretty, and one that has something about it that always makes you want to go round it again, no matter how often you see it. One of the most basic principles is to ensure that not all of

Lawns are often taken for granted, but they are in fact a very important element as they link all other features in the garden, forming the backdrop against which they are seen. In most conventional gardens a deep green weed-free lawn is the goal, but cottage gardeners generally prefer a more natural look. Many conserve buttercups and daisies, as does this gardener in Suffolk, and avoid using lawn fertilizer to encourage less common wild flowers. It is possible to buy wild flower lawn seed mixtures to sow instead of normal lawn grass seed when establishing a new lawn; these contain a fascinating blend of species suitable for all sorts of conditions.

the garden can be seen from the house, so that you are enticed out into it. Many cottage gardeners achieve this by having a small garden immediately round the house, with paths leading off behind groups of shrubs or a screen of climbers, or through archways that frame tantalizing glimpses of what lies beyond. And rather than make the whole garden visible from any one point, you can create much more 'mystery and curiosity' by dividing the garden up into compartments – gardens within the garden – each of which has its own separate character, and offers a different view to enjoy. Then, as you walk round the garden, the original visual trick is repeated; from each little garden that you discover you are lead on to another that you can't quite see until you get to it. You can vary the features that divide the compartments: use existing old stone walls if you are lucky enough to have them, or hedges, banks of shrubs or roses, outbuildings, or even espaliered fruit trees. You can increase the mystery by cutting 'peepholes' in hedges, giving a brief hint of a view to be enjoyed on the other side, which you must find a way round to. Even in a small garden, you can use the idea of compartments very successfully by keeping them small, and the intervening obstacles light or low. You can also open up views beyond the garden by lowering parts of the surrounding screen of shrubs or removing a tree to reveal a vista. Both these techniques have been used at Knapp Lane Farmhouse, Somerset, where although the garden surrounding the house is quite small, you can wander round very happily for hours, as there are so many different centres of interest to be investigated. Here the gardener has created a collection of gardens in miniature, each of which is a small replica of a full-sized garden that she would like to make.

The plants you choose can also contribute towards the curiosity value of a garden. Most cottage gardens include a good selection of flowers that appear and disappear within a relatively short time, which means there is always something new to be looked for. Bulbs are particularly useful in this respect; many cottage gardens include a few groups of the more unusual spring bulbs, like the snakeshead fritillary, as well as carpets of the commoner kinds, such as daffodils and bluebells. These might be followed by lilies, and as the summer progresses, *Amaryllis belladonna*, nerines, *Tricyrtis* (toad lily), or autumn-flowering colchicums. Unusual plants are a great encouragement to wander round the garden to see what is out, as is any new plant you have recently added but not yet seen flowering – more reasons for continuously adding to and changing a cottage garden to keep it interesting.

Here, a maze of narrow, winding paths overhung with plants are intended for exploring the garden at leisure. By wending between groups of plants, they add to the curiosity value of the garden by continuously leading you on to explore round the next bend.

Bibliography

The following books, some of which are no longer in print but which are occasionally available from second-hand booksellers, are specially useful further reading on the subject of cottage gardens, their plants and the people who originally occupied them.

BRICKELL, Christopher and SHARMAN, Fay, *The Vanishing Garden*, John Murray, London, 1986

COATS, Alice M., *Flowers and Their Histories*, A. & C. Black, London, 1968

COBBETT, William, *Cottage Economy*, 1821, Oxford University Press, Oxford, 1979

FISH, Margery, *Cottage Garden Flowers*, Faber & Faber, London, 1980

GENDERS, Roy, *Collecting Antique Plants*, Pelham Books, London, 1971

The Cottage Garden and the Old Fashioned Flowers, Pelham Books, London, 1983

The Cottage Garden Year, Croom Helm, Beckenham, Kent, 1986

GRIEVE, Mrs M., *A Modern Herbal*, Penguin, London, 1980

JABS, Carolyn, *The Heirloom Gardener*, Sierra Club, San Francisco, 1984

LACEY, Geraldine, *Creating Topiary*, Garden Art Press, Woodbridge, Suffolk, 1987

STUART THOMAS, Graham, *Old Shrub Roses*, rev. edn., J.M. Dent, London, 1979

Perennial Garden Plants, 2nd edn., J.M. Dent, London, 1982

VEREY, Rosemary, *Classic Garden Design*, rev. edn., John Murray, London, 1989

WILSON, C. Anne, *Food and Drink in Britain*, Penguin, London, 1984

Index

Acknowledgements

Our sincere thanks are due to all the many people who so generously allowed us to include their lovely gardens in this book:

Mr & Mrs D. Atkinson
Sir Francis & Lady Avery Jones
Peter Beales
Ronald Blyth
Dr & Mrs R. Brown
Miss S. Carter
Beth Chatto
Mrs Joan Cook
Mr & Mrs G. Garton
Mr & Mrs S. Gault
Mr & Mrs R. Gawen
Mr & Mrs J. Hubbard
Mrs Kathleen Hudson
Mr & Mrs M.G.D. Johnson
Mary Keen
Captain & Mrs G.A. Kitchin
Mr & Mrs F.W. Lambert

Mr & Mrs P. Lewis
Christopher Lloyd
Mr & Mrs R.R. Merton
Mrs S.M. Neville
Lord Northbourne
Mr & Mrs A. Norton
Audrey and Mary Pring
Mr & Mrs P. Rodgers
Mr & Mrs N.A. Slocock
Mr & Mrs A. Softly
John Southwell
Mr & Mrs D.A. Tolman
Mrs Gwladys Tonge
Rosemary Verey
Gillian Whaite
Mrs Susan Woodbridge
Mrs A.M. Wray

We would also like to thank the many more people who kindly volunteered their gardens, but which we were unable to include for reasons of time or space.

Thanks too, to Tony Lord for checking the copy, and making sure all the botanical plant names are the up-to-date versions and correctly set out. Lastly, to Felicity Luard who has done much more than just act as the book's editor – she was the vital link between garden owners, writer and photographer, putting us all in touch with each other, and co-ordinating what turned out to be an enormous amount of travel and research.